# CUSTOMER EQUITY

# CUSTOMER EQUITY

*Building and Managing Relationships as Valuable Assets*

Robert C. Blattberg
Gary Getz
Jacquelyn S. Thomas

HARVARD BUSINESS SCHOOL PRESS
BOSTON, MASSACHUSETTS

**Library of Congress Cataloging-in-Publication Data**
Blattberg, Robert C., 1942–
    Customer equity: building and managing relationships
    as valuable assets/Robert C. Blattberg, Gary Getz,
    Jacquelyn S. Thomas.
      p. cm.
    Includes index.
    ISBN 0-87584-764-1 (alk. paper)
    1. Relationship marketing.  2. Customer services—
Marketing.  3. Customer relations.  4. Customer loyalty.
I. Getz, Gary, 1955–   II. Thomas, Jacquelyn S., 1969–
III. Title.

HF5415.55 .B585 2001
658.8'12--dc21

                             00-069709

*To our spouses who provided inspiration during the creation of this manuscript:*

*Rebecca, Linda, and Terry*

# Contents

*Preface*  IX
*Acknowledgments*  XIII
*Customer Management: A Quiz*  XVII

### PART I
### A NEW MARKETING SYSTEM
**1.** Managing the Customer as an Asset  3
**2.** Cornerstones of Customer Equity  13

### PART II
### CUSTOMER STRATEGIES
**3.** Managing Customer Acquisition  35
**4.** Managing Customer Retention  67
**5.** Enhancing Customer Equity through Add-on Selling  95
**6.** Optimizing Customer Equity  125

### PART III
### MANAGING BY CUSTOMER EQUITY
**7.** The Marketing Mix  147
**8.** Customer Equity Accounting  161
**9.** Organizing for Customer Equity  173
**10.** The Future of Customer Equity  193

*Appendix: Issues in Computing Customer Equity*  209
*Notes*  213
*Index*  217
*About the Authors*  227

# Preface

We believe that advances in technology have rendered many traditional approaches to marketing obsolete, a point we discuss in chapter 2. We, and our friends at Harvard Business School Publishing, believe that the same is true for the world of books, and we have designed this book with that in mind. Several types of material—concepts, frameworks, and illustrative case studies, to name a few—lend themselves to inclusion in a book. Other relevant materials, such as analytic tools, formulas, and numeric examples, work better on the Internet, where they can be described in greater depth than is appropriate for the text of books. This also allows us to update and augment these materials as appropriate.

At several points in the book, we refer interested readers to our Web site at http://www.customerequity.com. This is a portal to explanations and examples not included in the text. Depending on the level of interest, we may also launch periodic updates, begin a discussion forum, and include links to customer equity resources. We also plan to use other Web capabilities as they emerge by adding new features now unforeseen. We hope that creating this multimedia environment will allow the interested reader to obtain greater depth on topics that are too specialized or detailed for the written text of the book. We look forward to your using the web site and providing suggestions and ideas to us through e-mail.

## Who Should Read This Book?

If you want to build your company's customer assets for optimal financial performance, then this book is for you.

*CEOs and Chief Strategy Officers:* Disruptive changes in the world of market interactions put your company's future at risk. Rapid action not only can overcome the risk but also can position you and your company as the Wanamaker, Schwab, Sloan, or Bezos of your industry. Part I of the book, "A New Marketing System," describes these changes, and Part III, "Managing by Customer Equity," talks about the changes in strategy, organization, and metrics that you must make to succeed.

*CFOs and accounting executives:* Better diagnostics lead to better decisions. Customer equity's precise metrics help you evaluate your business more effectively and improve performance. It is the activity-based management of your company's marketplace. You may find chapter 8 on customer equity accounting and the latter parts of chapters 3, 4, and 5, which describe key diagnostics, of particular interest.

*Marketing and sales executives:* Customer equity is the way that successful marketers will view their markets. It provides a new framework and model for structuring your go-to-market activities, links those activities to useful metrics, and helps you to make better marketing decisions and evaluate their results. You should give particular attention to chapter 7's advice on using customer equity to manage the marketing mix.

*Chief Information Officers:* The move to customer equity marketing places information management at the center of market success, if your organization can meet the challenges of gathering, integrating, and interpreting the needed information. Be sure to look at chapter 9's discussion of required skills and processes, and the sections of chapters 3 through 6 that focus on data management requirements.

*Chief Technology Officers:* Technology and product development play important roles in maximizing the value of a company's customer assets. See the discussions in chapters 3 through 5 on how you need to rethink your product portfolio to drive customer acquisition and retention, and add-on selling.

*Human resources executives and knowledge officers:* Managing an organization to maximize the asset value of its customer relationships will require new skill sets, processes, leadership behaviors, cultural norms, organizing structures, and reward systems. The organizing implications of customer equity are addressed throughout the book, most notably in chapter 9.

*Account executives, public relations specialists, alumni officers, political representatives, clinical trials managers, not-for-profit managers, recruiters—in fact, anyone serving a valuable constituency:* As you progress through this book, you will learn the strategies and tactics of customer equity along with the how-to of executing this new marketing system to maximize the value of the constituencies you serve. As a practitioner, you may be particularly interested in the details available at our Web site, www.customerequity.com.

Robert C. Blattberg
Gary Getz
Jacquelyn S. Thomas

# ACKNOWLEDGMENTS

This book was a twenty-five year journey. It began in 1975 when Robert Blattberg became aware of the power and elegance of the concept of lifetime value of a customer through Baldwin-Cooke, a small company in Morton Grove, Illinois. Baldwin-Cooke's CEO, Tom Nichol, managed the business by optimizing the lifetime value of his customers through acquisition and retention processes. It was contrary to mass marketing, whose focus was treating customers as transactions (short-term sales) and reaching and marketing to customers at a low cost. Lifetime value of a customer made the customer an asset one should manage.

The concept incubated until 1991 when Professor Blattberg gave the Wroe Alderson Lecture at The Wharton School. He chose the topic of customer equity and began to lay out some of the concepts used in this book. In 1996 he and Professor John Deighton of Harvard published a paper on customer equity, which was the first academic contribution to mention customer equity.

However, it was not until the collaboration with Gary Getz and Jacquelyn Thomas that this idea became more than just a concept whose genesis was in lifetime value. They helped create the framework and understanding of customer equity as a management concept that transcends marketing and becomes the basis for a radical change in the management of the firm around the customer.

This book represents the beginning of research on customer equity. We like to think of it as an evolutionary process, which will require scientific research to develop concrete knowledge of how customers are acquired, retained, and enhanced. This book is designed to provide those interested in a customer-centric view of the firm with an understanding of how it can become a holistic system that serves as the strategic cornerstone of a firm.

The authors would like to thank several individuals without whose assistance this book could not have been written. Lisa Robbins worked tirelessly with us to shape our prose and help us to create a manuscript that was worthy of consideration as a book. And her daughter, Emma, put up with the postponement of her second birthday party for a week so that Lisa could whip the first manuscript into shape in time for our submittal deadline. Above and beyond the call, indeed.

Kirsten Sandberg, our executive editor at Harvard Business School Press, provided invaluable guidance on tone, emphasis, and structure and inspired the thought of turning an initial manuscript that tried to reach from concepts all the way to calculations into a more tightly focused book complemented by a Web site. Erin Korey, editorial coordinator, Amanda Gardner, manuscript editor, Jennifer Hill, and Sharon Rice, all at the Press, steered us through the complexities of the production process. They played their roles with relentless good cheer—their encouraging e-mails played a big role in keeping our spirits up, particularly during the final push.

Several individuals at Integral, Inc., and its parent company, Analysis Group, Inc., assisted our efforts. Bruce Stangle, Martha Samuelson, and Norm Gorin of Analysis Group provided both moral and financial support. Mark Pelofsky of Integral lent project management skills and led the development of several case studies that appear in the book. Aparna Upadhyay and Gail Williams drafted case studies, and Aparna also managed the assembly of the revised manuscript. Professor Luis Huete, an Integral faculty affiliate, allowed us to use company interview information in our case studies that he and Mark Pelofsky had jointly developed.

Finally, we acknowledge the tremendous debt that we owe our spouses. They put up with ruined vacations, foregone weekends, and constant talk about what one spouse started to call "the b-word" for far too long. Without their steadfast support, guidance, and no little sacrifice, we would not have had the opportunity to bring the customer equity message to a broader audience.

Bob Blattberg acknowledges John Deighton, who developed the original concepts of customer equity. Thanks to Lynn Chaney, who has been a partner at Blattberg, Chaney for fifteen years and who was instrumental in much of our early work in direct marketing and provided assistance in some of the drafts of this manuscript. To Tom Sarnowski of Blattberg, Chaney, who has provided numerous statistical analyses of direct marketing data and helped build models of customer lifetime value. To Dipak Jain and Lakshman Krishnamurthi, who provided support and encouragement at the Kellogg School of Management at Northwestern University. To Michael Lewis and Vishal Singh, currently doctoral students at the Kellogg School of Management at Northwestern University, who provided assistance in creating examples and research used in this book. Finally, to Jakki Thomas, who entered the project and provided energy and discipline to ensure the completion of this manuscript.

Gary Getz acknowledges the tremendous role that Lou Stern, the noted marketing channel strategist, has had in shaping both his thinking and his character, and also thanks Fred Sturdivant, Dave Reibstein, Ben Shapiro, Paul Green, Subrata Sen, Glen Urban, and Earl Sasser for the lessons they imparted on marketing and customer management. Many thanks to Bob Blattberg for extending the opportunity to join this project, and to Jakki Thomas for both her tremendous contributions and her calming influence. Former colleagues Chris Tchen and Dave Crosswhite provided useful critiques and great examples. Ed Tuttle and the other partners of Integral picked up the slack when "book writing" activities took time away from the firm's immediate needs. Bonnie Porter Mitchell provided crucial early encouragement that has not been forgotten. Finally, thanks to Kathy Leslie, who commented on drafts, compiled bibliographies, lent moral support, and did a hundred other things to make this book a reality.

Jacquelyn Thomas gives thanks first and foremost to God for guiding her through this process. Jakki would also like to thank Bob Blattberg and Gary Getz for including her in this project. Special thanks are also extended to Liz Caracciolo and Elizabeth Halkos, Emory M.B.A. students, for their support and case-writing contributions. Their dedication and commitment are greatly appreciated. Many thanks to Professor Elizabeth Odders-White and Professor Peter Henry for their continued moral support throughout this project. Last but not least, Jakki would like to acknowledge her family for their endless support and inspiration—follow your passions and success will follow.

# Customer Management:
# A Quiz

Before you begin, test your knowledge of customer management by answering the following questions. To check your answers, refer to the chapters noted.

1. The bottom line of your income statement tells you best whether your customer management efforts are working. True or false? Chapter 8

2. What's most important in maximizing the value of customers to a company: new customer acquisition, customer retention, or add-on selling of additional products to current customers? Chapter 6

3. Customer asset value can only be calculated using sophisticated mathematical models. True or false? Chapter 6

4. Mass marketing is the most efficient marketing approach. True or false? Chapters 1 and 3

5. Companies should set a goal of retaining 100 percent of their customers. True or false? Chapter 4

6. Improved customer satisfaction translates directly into more profitable customer relationships. True or false? Chapter 4

7. A company can focus on customer value or brand equity, but not both. True or false? Chapter 10

8. You should offer your most loyal customers the best prices. True or false? Chapter 4

9. The maximum success rate of companies at acquiring new customers depends on the industry they are in and can't be exceeded or changed. True or false? Chapter 7

10. All customers should be targeted for add-on selling of products and services they aren't buying now. True or false? Chapter 5

11. A company's product portfolio plays a key role in building the value of its customer portfolio. True or false? Chapters 3, 4, and 5

12. Extensive databases on customer behavior are the required starting point for calculating and managing customer value. True or false? Chapters 2 and 6

13. Customers are valuable financial assets that should be acquired and developed in ways similar to the way in which a company's more tangible assets are managed. True or false? Chapter 1

14. Tangible assets such as manufacturing facilities have measurable and manageable life cycles, but customer relationship assets do not. True or false? Chapter 2

15. Who is responsible for maximizing customer asset value: Marketing, Information Services, or Accounting? Chapter 9

16. Will the explosion in the availability of customer behavioral data make customer management easier or harder? Chapter 10

17. The lifetime value of a customer calculated at the time of acquisition determines the strategy that should be used to manage the customer relationship. True or false? Chapters 7 and 8

18. Customer acquisition, retention, and add-on selling change in relative importance as product categories mature. True or false? Chapters 2 and 7

19. To manage customer assets most effectively, should companies organize their marketing efforts around customer segments or

around customer acquisition, customer retention, and add-on selling? Chapter 9

20. A firm's marketing mix for recently acquired customers should be different from that for customers who have dealt with the firm for many years. True or false? Chapter 7

21. Does acquiring customers through aggressive introductory promotions and pricing build or destroy the value of the customer portfolio over the long term? Chapters 3 and 4

22. Firms should focus their customer acquisition efforts on prospects whose lifetime value exceeds the average of the current customer portfolio. True or false? Chapter 3

23. Switching behavior driven by the availability of data on the Internet, along with privacy concerns, makes the concept of customer asset management irrelevant to online businesses. True or false? Chapters 4 and 10

24. We can say that we have acquired a customer when the customer buys something from us. True or false? Chapter 3

25. Customers who buy more types of things from us remain customers longer than those who do not. True or false? Chapter 5

# CUSTOMER EQUITY

# PART I

---

# A NEW
# MARKETING
# SYSTEM

# I

# MANAGING THE
# CUSTOMER AS AN ASSET

CUSTOMER EQUITY's basic premise is straightforward: The customer is a financial asset that companies and organizations should measure, manage, and maximize just like any other asset. Customer equity management is a dynamic, integrative marketing system that uses financial valuation techniques and data about customers to optimize the acquisition of, retention of, and selling of additional products to a firm's customers, and that maximizes the value to the company of the customer relationship throughout its life cycle. Although many of the concepts that underlay customer equity management (such as customer retention marketing and customer lifetime value measurement) are not new, the way that the customer equity approach unifies and moves beyond them is.

In the last two decades, managerial trends have tended to focus on either cost management or revenue growth. Customer equity management balances the two, creating market-based growth while carefully evaluating the profitability and return on investment (ROI) of marketing investment.

But customer equity management is more than just a method for calculating the asset value of customer relationships. It is a total marketing system. It requires integrative business strategies: Firms will need to develop strategies that simultaneously manage products and customers throughout the customer life cycle and that reframe brand and product strategies within the context of their effects on customer equity.

In addition, the customer equity framework changes the way a business allocates resources and efforts. Today, most marketing functions allocate resources by product line. With a customer orientation, the customer life cycle determines how managers distribute resources. As we will describe in chapter 9, companies that adopt customer equity management also need to build organizations, processes, and performance measures that work together to maximize customer asset value.

Charles Schwab offers an excellent example. In its early days, Schwab focused on customer acquisition by providing self-reliant investors with a value-priced alternative to full-service brokerage houses. The company invested little in understanding its customers' needs and wants at anything beyond the aggregate level:

> Although Schwab contended that it made a significant commitment to better understanding its customer base, its reputation for customer knowledge was poor. "Fidelity used to know more about Schwab's customers than Schwab did," remarked one insider in 1996. "What they had built were transaction systems. What they need is customer information."[1]

Later, in response to competitive pressures, Schwab began to apply the two other levers of customer equity: add-on selling (selling more to its existing customers) and retention (keeping existing customers). It expanded its offerings to develop multiple relationships with customers who stayed longer with Schwab. Schwab's OneSource mutual fund marketplace provided a multibranded alternative that appealed to more investors than did the single-branded mutual fund offerings of brokerage houses and investment companies. As one expert noted, Schwab outflanked the competition by creating a "best of breed marketplace" that gave unbiased access to the funds of multiple providers.[2] The firm captured a higher share of customers' investment assets and raised retention rates.

## Benefits of Customer Equity

Organizations that use customer equity as a marketing system benefit because they can do the following:

- Compute the asset value of customers to make informed decisions regarding investments in acquisition, retention, and add-on selling

- Adjust marketing investment levels as customer relationships move through their dynamic life cycles

- Organize processes and structures around acquisition, retention, and add-on selling to maximize the profitability of each over the customer life cycle

- Address the "whole customer," who buys and uses a broad range of services and products

- Utilize customer interactions to reinforce relationships and acquire new customers

Managing the customer as an asset is more critical to a firm's success than ever before for three reasons. First, marketers who take an asset-based view of the customer make better decisions than those who limit themselves to product, brand, or transaction views. Second, today's computing technology makes precise customer asset management possible. Companies can now efficiently obtain and process the information they need to understand customer equity. Finally, changes in market conditions, driven by advances in information systems, communications, and production, will help companies that understand and manage the value of each individual customer to overtake, and then displace, mass marketers.

## Making Better Decisions

Once the concept of maximizing customer asset value is pointed out, it seems obvious. Yet most firms do not act as if they consider customers as assets. Instead they maximize product line or transaction profitability. Product-line maximizers use traditional accounting measures and product management as tools. By focusing on product and transaction profitability to the exclusion of customer asset value, they often increase near-term profits but forfeit longer-term prosperity.

A look at General Motors's strategy in the late 1970s helps to show the difference. The goal of GM's management was to increase short-term profits and shareholder returns. Based on financial analyses that showed that small cars were relatively unprofitable, they de-emphasized the small cars in the product line in favor of larger, more profitable vehicles.[3] Not surprisingly, the strategy worked. GM's profits showed immediate improvement. At the same time GM was pruning its product line, however, Japanese automakers were offering smaller, higher-quality, lower-priced cars than GM. Small cars served as a mechanism for acquiring young first-time buyers.[4] When these same customers began to purchase larger cars (as they evolved through the customer life cycle), they continued to buy Japanese cars.[5] GM inadvertently created a generation of young American consumers who grew up buying Japanese and German cars.

GM did not practice customer equity management. Even at low profits, the sale of high-quality, low-priced cars was critical to its long-term franchise value. It is ironic that the heirs to Alfred Sloan's brilliant product-ladder strategy could lose sight of the importance of, and linkage between, customer acquisition and customer retention in the automobile business. GM's product management strategy led to a decrease in its market share of about 15 percent (from approximately 45 percent to 30 percent) over twenty years.

Viewing customers as assets also differs significantly from treating brand equity as the primary marketing asset. Although the two are not mutually exclusive, they have different objectives. Brand orientation provides a clear goal for marketing activities: to maximize a brand's total revenues and extract the greatest possible return from brand investment. The customer asset orientation focuses on a firm's entire future net income stream across brands and services. It does not view the customer only through the narrow aperture of the brand.

As illustrated in table 1-1, companies that take a customer asset approach do things differently than their brand equity–based counterparts do. Brand-oriented companies focus on product quality and customer service as a means to build the brand's perceived value. They advertise to position the brand and worry that promotions will dilute its value. In many brand-oriented companies, product development focuses on line extensions meant to leverage the brand name into new arenas. These companies pay substantial attention to how a strong brand can provide power in a battle against competitors within a multilevel distribution system.

In a customer equity–oriented company, these same elements work much differently. Quality and service act as customer retention tools. Advertising messages serve to build affinity between the customer and the company, and promotions function as strategic events designed to drive repeat buying and increase lifetime relationship value. New products present opportunities to cross-sell existing customers. Whether

**Table 1-1**
Features of the Brand Equity and Customer Equity Approaches

| Marketing Activity | Brand Equity | Customer Equity |
|---|---|---|
| Product and service quality | Create strong customer preference | Create high customer retention rates |
| Advertising | Create brand image and position | Create customer affinity |
| Promotions | Deplete brand equity | Create repeat buying and enhance lifetime value |
| Product development | Use brand name to create flankers and related products | Acquire products to sell to the installed customer base |
| Segmentation | Customer characteristics and benefit segmentation | Behavioral segmentation based on customer database |
| Channels of distribution | Multistage distribution system | Direct distribution to customer |
| Customer service | Enhance brand image | Create customer affinity |

the company sells directly to customers or uses a multilayer channel system, direct knowledge of individual customers and their buying behaviors is its lifeblood.

## Why Customer Equity?

There are two fundamental reasons for companies to move to a customer equity approach. First, several critical new technologies are converging to make customer asset–based management feasible. Second, these same technological capabilities, along with other changes in how markets work in today's turbulent business environment, are making it a requirement to manage marketing to maximize the value of a company's customer assets.

### Because You Can

Customer equity management is now possible because of intersecting advances in four areas: affordable information technology, low-cost communications, sophisticated statistical modeling, and flexible fulfillment.

Customer equity depends on technology because it requires the ability to build and use databases of customer purchases. Computing costs are continuing to decline to the point at which small businesses can have computing power sufficient to manage large databases at a fraction of what it would have cost in the 1980s. The ability to work with large, sophisticated databases is improving; software to manage customer relationships now exists, and its capabilities are expanding.

The rapid growth of the Internet as a medium for targeted communication allows firms to reach and communicate with customers at less than one-hundredth of the cost of more traditional techniques. Using direct marketing through the mail costs anywhere from $400 to $1,000 per 1,000 mailings. Communication through the Internet to customers equipped with e-mail is virtually free, and the speed of transmission allows customers to retrieve communications almost instantaneously. Firms have access to their preferred customers at costs that early direct marketers could only dream about, combined with unprecedented ability to tailor messages to individual recipients and provide electronic coupons to selected prospects. Furthermore, software is being created using artificial intelligence to develop automated two-way communications with customers based on their specific responses to queries.

In addition, technologies ranging from checkout scanning to Internet cookies are making it increasingly possible to track customers' buying behaviors. Now companies can predict future consumer behavior using the best possible indicator: current behavior. Instead of relying on focus groups and surveys to ask customers what they want (or think they want), firms can examine actual purchase histories. As more and more online customers grant companies permission to use their personal data in return for anticipating needs, this trend toward greater availability of behavioral data should only accelerate.

Companies must use advanced analytical tools to turn these data into insights. Techniques such as collaborative filtering track customer buying patterns and make recommendations about which types of books, movies, or other products the customer might want to purchase. Modeling methods for determining customers' sensitivity to price and responsiveness to offers, central to improving the efficiency of marketing offers, have become both more sophisticated and more available.

### Because You Must

Figure 1-1 highlights several disruptive changes to the world of marketing that make customer equity management a necessity, along with the underlying trends that drive these disruptions.

Trends                     Disruptions

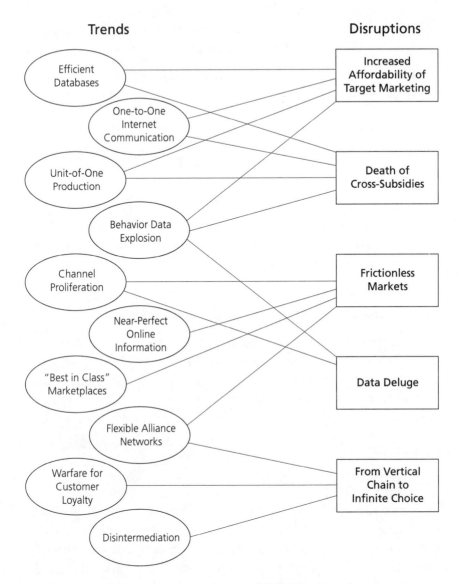

**Figure 1-1** Disruptive Changes and Their Underlying Trends

- For the reasons mentioned in the prior section, information-based targeted marketing is becoming more efficient and effective than blanketed mass marketing.

- As one result, mass marketing strategies that achieve targeted profits by counting on more-profitable customers to subsidize less-profitable ones will fail as the more attractive customers are stolen away by competitors' targeted acquisition efforts.

- As customers gain near-perfect information on their alternatives, switching barriers (discussed in chapter 4) are dropping dramatically.

- Companies that use the deluge of available data on customer purchase behavior are acquiring new customers, retaining existing customers, and cross-selling more effectively than those who do not, and can link their insights with cost data to do so efficiently as well.

- Companies can no longer depend on orderly vertical channel systems to control customers' buying behaviors.

In a world characterized by these five forces, companies that understand the asset value of each customer, and that tailor their marketing efforts (and their costs) to acquire and sustain the highest-value assets, will trump less-focused mass marketers.

## Measurement: The Core of Customer Equity

Managing customers as assets requires measuring, managing, and maximizing them. Total Quality Management taught production and operations managers that in order to manage a process you must measure it. Marketing has always been weak on measurement. Marketing research is the closest marketers usually come to measurement; however, such research is far removed from the actual measurement of sales and profits. Customer equity provides more direct measures, including the customer equity flow statement described in chapter 8.

Managing what is measured becomes easier because decisions are no longer opinion based, but fact based. With specific information in hand, managers can optimize the firm's marketing mix across the customer life cycle, as we discuss in chapter 7, creating different mixes for new customers, inactive customers, and long-time core customers. All the while, because the customer equity approach is financially driven, the firm maximizes customer asset value.

## What's New in This Book

This book presents several new concepts and integrates many existing customer marketing approaches. Figure 1-2 shows the major elements of the customer equity model. Customer equity management is different from "marketing" as most companies practice it. If you're not

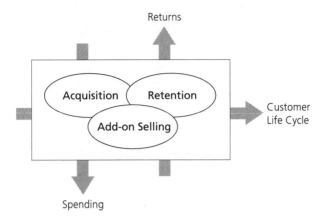

**Figure 1-2** The Customer Equity Model

convinced, test your existing marketing approach against the criteria in box 1-1.

We emphasize six basic changes to marketing strategy:

1. Marketing strategy, tactics, and execution become customer-centric, not product-centric.

2. The firm manages a customer life cycle. The marketing mix varies by stage in the customer life cycle.

3. The firm manages a portfolio of customers balanced across acquisition, retention, and add-on selling stages.

4. The marketing output of the firm is quantifiable. Marketing is managed using the appropriate customer equity measures, and costs are balanced against financial returns.

5. The firm communicates changes in the asset value of its customers through customer equity flow statements. The firm measures its customer assets through lifetime value.

6. The firm organizes around customer acquisition, retention, and add-on selling.

This book does not repeat the vast literature on customer relationship management, database marketing, and customer satisfaction. Instead it uses, and unifies, these concepts within the customer equity framework.

**Box 1-1**  Criteria for Marketing System Performance

As you think about the approach that your company currently uses to address its markets, how well does it satisfy the criteria that were used to develop customer equity as a marketing system?

- Does it drive *acquisition?* Specifically, is this approach one that gives your company great power in attracting new customers to its offerings?

- Does it drive *retention?* Is this a particularly strong way to keep customers once you have them?

- How useful is the approach in creating *add-on sales?*

- Does this marketing system help your company to *optimize* the efforts and resources it expends on acquisition, retention, and add-on selling? Providing a fact-based method for optimizing these elements of your marketing system is a central feature of the customer equity approach.

- Is the method in question *customer focused?* Does it operate from the outside market in, or from a company's internal economics—or even from its established brands—out?

- If you use a given approach, can you *tailor and target?* Can you provide different offerings and messages to different segments, subsegments, and even individuals? Can you focus your efforts on more attractive segments and customers and away from less attractive ones? Can you even know or find out the difference?

- Is the approach static or *dynamic?* That is, does it help you to manage customer relationship life cycles and portfolios of customer types as they shift over time, or does it provide you only with the ability to manage your business at a specific point in time?

# 2

---

# CORNERSTONES OF
# CUSTOMER EQUITY

Customer equity management depends on four cornerstones to maximize the value of the customer as a financial asset:

- Managing the customer life cycle

- Exploiting the power of databases

- Quantifying customer value precisely

- Optimizing the mix of customer acquisition, retention, and add-on selling

These cornerstones of customer equity management provide the structure a company needs for targeting, cultivating, and reaping customer value. If any one is missing, the marketing system will weaken. A company may choose to implement these practices in stages, but in the long term it must adopt all four to succeed.

## Customer Life Cycle

Customer equity management recognizes that customer–firm relationships, like all relationships, evolve over time. Prospects, new buyers, and long-time customers do not have the same needs, and as their relationships with a company change, so do their expectations and

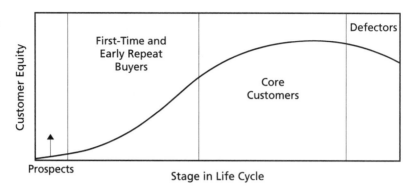

**Figure 2-1**   The Customer Life Cycle

behavior. The concept of the customer life cycle provides a framework for understanding and managing these differences.

Figure 2-1 shows the five customer life cycle stages: prospects, first-time buyers, early repeat buyers, core customers, and defectors.

### Stage 1: Prospects

Prospects are not yet customers, but they represent potential value. (Highly qualified prospects are particularly important.) Firms need to manage them as they would initial customers. That said, prospects pose unique problems: Should they be offered prices below those given to existing customers? What level of sales effort should they receive? What type of communication should be offered to them regarding the quality and the value of the firm's offerings?

These questions are very important, often in ways that firms do not expect. For example, marketing communications that create overly high expectations among prospects adversely affect retention once these customers have made a few purchases and been disappointed. A firm that makes this mistake ends up with high acquisition rates but low retention rates. Too few firms recognize that the marketing tactics used during the prospect stage have repercussions throughout the customer–firm relationship.

During the prospect stage the consumer develops an initial set of expectations about a product or service. If these expectations exceed the customer's product-quality cutoff, the customer will make a first purchase. The quality of products that the customer already uses, along with information about the new product provided by the firm through its marketing communications, determines his or her product-quality cutoff. The consumer also considers price; the product or service must meet a value cutoff as well.

## Stage 2: First-Time Buyers

Customers move into this stage after making one purchase. These newly acquired customers usually have the lowest retention rates within a firm's customer base. Although they have signaled that the firm's products meet their specifications, they are still in the evaluation stage. They need to learn whether the products and customer service levels meet their expectations.

If the product meets expectations and remains above the quality cutoff, the customer will continue to purchase and be retained as long as the product's value is maintained. If the product does not meet expectations, the customer will stop purchasing and defect. During these early repeat purchases, just one product failure (in which the product falls below the customer's quality cutoff) generally will cause defection.

Some products and services have long purchase cycles, which make repeat buying by customers at this stage less important. In industries characterized by shorter purchase cycles and frequent repurchasing, such as air express services, supplies for industrial maintenance, and consumer packaged goods, the potential future value of first-time buyers significantly affects customer equity. For these businesses, converting customers into repeat buyers and core customers is very important.

## Stage 3: Early Repeat Buyers

Customers advance to this stage after making one repeat purchase. These customers are more likely to buy again than first-time buyers, and sales per customer increase as they gain confidence with the firm. However, although two to three repeat purchases indicate satisfaction with the product, these early repeat buyers are still evaluating the relationship. If the firm provides poor service or the product does not meet expectations, they may defect.

Firms rarely identify this stage in the customer life cycle. Early repeat buyers may not be as vulnerable as first-time buyers, but they still have lower retention rates than core customers who have repeat-purchased many times, and must be managed accordingly.

### Stage 4: Core Customers

Customers enter the core customer stage after they begin to repeat-purchase regularly. The firm's product or service meets their required specifications and value. Unless a major problem arises with the purchasing process, these customers rarely reevaluate the firm's product. An occasional product failure will not automatically cause defection; numerous positive experiences serve as a basis for the customer's expectations and carry him or her through the disappointing experience. In fact, at this stage, expectations change only slightly each time the customer uses the product. Only in bid businesses or at contract renewals do these customers evaluate their decisions systematically.

The core customer stage has the highest retention rates and the highest sales per customer. These customers are special and should be treated as such. Ironically, some firms de-emphasize their core customers because of these high retention rates. Management does not see these customers as problems and so pays less attention to them.

### Stage 5: Core Defectors

At some point, core customers become willing to switch suppliers or brands. Several factors can cause this, such as new competing products or services, a customer service problem that was not rectified properly, or boredom.

Some customer defection is controllable; some is not. When external events cause defection, a firm's policies cannot influence the decision. Each firm must determine the extent to which external events cause defection. If external factors are too prevalent, then retention investments to avoid defections will not be effective.

A firm can reactivate a defector if the underlying problem is recognized and rectified. Often, firms fail to identify defectors and do not act to bring them back into the fold.

### Evidence of the Customer Life Cycle

How do we know that customer life cycles exist? Evidence comes from two sources: research on new product acceptance, and *recency, frequency, and monetary* (RFM) *analysis*, a widely accepted measurement tool in direct marketing.

## New Product Acceptance

In the 1970s, several journals published research on new-product acceptance models.[1] These models began with consumer trial, induced through product advertising or some form of promotion. The consumer tried the product, and if it met expectations in terms of quality and price, then the consumer continued purchasing. After several purchases, the repeat-buying probability (retention rate) stabilized. Generally speaking, the highest sales for a frequently repeat-purchased product occurred in the first several months of the product's existence. Sales then would decline and ultimately plateau as the product reached a "steady state" of new buyers and repeat buyers.

These new-product acceptance models showed that during the first few purchases, the customer had a lower probability of repeat buying than after four or five purchases. The models used the term *depth of repeat* to describe the number of times the customer repeat-purchased. This depth of repeat can be plotted against customer retention rates. Figure 2-2 shows the resulting pattern: As the number of purchases climbs, the retention rate increases. This pattern is fundamental to the concept of the customer life cycle. It charts in basic terms the direction in which successful customer–firm relationships progress.

## Recency, Frequency, and Monetary Analysis

Other evidence of the customer life cycle comes from the use of RFM analysis in direct marketing. RFM analysis uses buying behavior to categorize customers into cells, each of which is targeted and marketed to

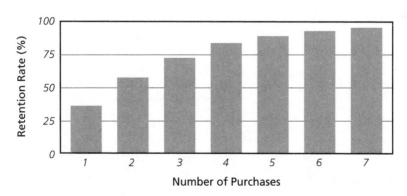

**Figure 2-2**    Retention Rate by Number of Purchases

differently. (For a more detailed description of RFM analysis, see chapter 4.) Table 2-1 is an RFM matrix for a specific direct-mail retailer. Based on experience, this retailer has determined which RFM classifications fall into which stages of the customer life cycle.

How does an RFM matrix imply a customer life cycle? The argument is similar to that regarding depth of repeat. The sample RFM matrix in table 2-2 reveals that first-time buyers have a much lower probability of repeat purchase and a much higher probability of defection. As customers increase their purchasing frequency, the likelihood of defection decreases and the probability of making a purchase on the next purchase occasion goes up.

**Table 2-1**
RFM Targeting Strategy

| Frequency | Monetary | Recency in Months | | | | |
| | | 0–6 | 7–12 | 13–18 | 19–24 | 25+ |
|---|---|---|---|---|---|---|
| 1 | <$50 | **First-Time Customers** | **Low Targeting Value** | | | |
| 1 | >$50 | | | | | |
| 2 | <$50 | **Early Repeat Customers** | **Non–Core Defectors** | | | |
| 2 | >$50 | | | | | |
| 3 | <$50 | | | | | |
| 3 | >$50 | | | | | |
| 4 | <$100 | **Core (High-Value) Customers** | **Core Defectors** | | | |
| 4 | >$100 | | | | | |
| 5+ | <$150 | | | | | |
| 5+ | >$150 | | | | | |

**Table 2-2**
Recency, Frequency, and Monetary Analysis

| | Months Since Last Purchase | | | | |
| | 0–6 | 7–12 | 13–18 | 19–24 | 25+ |
|---|---|---|---|---|---|
| One-time buyer, under $50 | 0.05 | 0.035 | 0.015 | 0.01 | 0.005 |
| One-time buyer, over $50 | 0.06 | 0.040 | 0.025 | 0.01 | 0.005 |
| Two-time buyer, under $50 | 0.08 | 0.065 | 0.035 | 0.02 | 0.010 |
| Two-time buyer, over $50 | 0.10 | 0.080 | 0.050 | 0.03 | 0.015 |
| Three-time buyer (or more) | 0.15 | 0.100 | 0.080 | 0.05 | 0.020 |

**Table 2-3**
Zap Online Inc. Subscriber Case

| Customer Description | Average Duration of Customer | Number of Subscribers | Average Customer Churn Rate | Subscriber Churn |
|---|---|---|---|---|
| New customers (Zap Newbies) | 0–4 months | 200,000 | 30% | 60,000 |
| Early repeat buyers (Budding Zap Loyalists) | 4–12 months | 400,000 | 15% | 60,000 |
| Core customers (Zap loyalists) | 12+ months | 600,000 | 5% | 30,000 |
| Totals | | 1,200,000 | 12.50% | |

## Zap Online, Inc.

The example of Zap Online, an Internet service provider (not an actual company, but an amalgam of several), helps to demonstrate the customer life cycle empirically. Because Zap Online was worried about customer defections, it commissioned a study to determine defection, or churn rates, and their causes. Table 2-3 shows that the churn rate is highest for customers with zero to four months' duration with the company, lower for those with four to twelve months, and lowest for customers with greater than twelve months' duration.

Reasons for defecting were also significantly different across life cycle stages (table 2-4). For new customers, the primary causes were poor response time and price. For customers who were in the early stages of the life cycle (four to twelve months), the primary causes were response time and customer service issues. For core customers (longer than twelve months), it was technical issues.

These data and research findings led management to identify the two areas that they must fix: response time for customers who are in the early life cycle stage, and technical issues associated with connections and Internet downloading. Price, which was the primary concern among new customers, was not an issue to long-term customers or to early-life-stage customers. Zap decided to keep prices high.

### Implications of the Customer Life Cycle

The key lesson from Zap is that the customer life cycle influences the design of the marketing mix (which we discuss in chapter 7). Briefly, the

**Table 2-4**
Reasons for Customer Defection at Zap

| Top Reasons for Discontinuing Zap's Service | Zap Newbies (%) | Budding Zap Loyalists (%) | Zap Loyalists (%) |
|---|---|---|---|
| CUSTOMER SERVICE | | | |
| Poor response time | 33 | 65 | 22 |
| Poor technical feedback | 8 | 13 | 5 |
| Other (e.g., rudeness, lack of response) | 4 | 2 | 1 |
| TECHNICAL ISSUES | | | |
| Speed to connect | 4 | 7 | 20 |
| Ability to download from the Internet | 12 | 5 | 43 |
| PRICE | | | |
| Increase in current rate | 21 | 4 | 5 |
| Lower competitor rates | 18 | 3 | 4 |

marketing mix differs significantly by stage in the customer life cycle. Prospect marketing is generally focused on awareness generation and trial promotions, whereas core customer marketing is focused on retention vehicles, pricing, and reinforcing (attitudinal) advertising. The firm must develop unique marketing mix strategies by life cycle segment.

The firm must also have the ability to balance the number of customers being acquired with the number defecting. This requires determining the number of customers in each stage of the customer life cycle and anticipating their migration paths. If the firm has too aggressive an acquisition program and many early repeat buyers who defect, the company will have significant cash flow problems. Internet firms, particularly e-tailers, have learned this lesson the hard way. Firms can track the number of customers in each stage of the life cycle to determine what the likely customer purchasing patterns will be and what the firm's cash flow will be. This becomes a powerful planning tool because the firm can analyze future sales patterns at a much more fundamental level than by simply predicting future sales levels based on past aggregate revenues.

## The Power of Databases

To manage assets that change over time, companies need to track them and to understand how they change. To manage customer assets, therefore, companies need customer databases. Without the insights that databases allow in predicting future customer behavior, managers would find it very difficult indeed to make the strategic and tactical choices they face when optimizing acquisition, retention, and add-on selling.

Customer databases have a broad range of applications. Hotel chains use customer databases to tailor their service approaches and communications, thereby increasing customer retention. Supermarkets use them to structure their preferred card programs, which drive higher revenues through price discrimination. Spiegel uses its database to build tailored promotions and design individualized product offerings, increasing add-on sales. And no-fee credit card companies model consumer behavior to target their mailings, which saves money and helps to acquire more attractive customers. All increase their customer equity as a result.

The use of databases for targeting and analysis is powerful because it enables a shift from third-degree segmentation (or self-selection) to first-degree segmentation: the creation of individually tailored offerings based on customer characteristics and behavior. Furthermore, it employs observation rather than inference. Inferences about customer needs and preferences are often useful, but observed shopping and purchasing behavior far more powerfully predicts future buying behavior. Once they can predict future buying behaviors, the hotels, supermarkets, credit card companies, and Internet marketers of this world can take action to "mass customize" every element of the marketing mix for markets of one.

In the past, database marketing functioned as a tactically driven system for obtaining customer data and designing acquisition programs aimed at selected customer groups. One-on-one marketing, which directs tailored offerings to individual customers, pushes database marketing a step further. It uses databases to capture the interactions between a firm and its customers at each point in time, and uses data analysis to search for patterns in these interactions. These patterns point to the most attractive potential customers and provide clues to help tailor products, pricing, and promotions. At its best, database marketing provides insights across the categories that customers buy, allowing companies to understand and sell to the "whole customer" rather than the customer seen only through the narrow view of their own products and brands.

Of course, the use of customer database marketing does have limitations. Its software and hardware requirements have made it expensive to set up. It often demands new skills and organizations, from new analytical and decision-making skills in sales and marketing to a revamped information-systems organization that can support entirely new classes of users. (Chapter 9 discusses the organizational requirements for successful implementation of customer equity.) Because of real-world limits on the data that systems and technicians can supply, there usually is a gap between the information that marketers need and the information they realistically can expect to receive. Database marketing also depends greatly on data quality. (Observational data are powerful. Corrupted observational data are powerfully misleading.) It depends, too, on the quality of analysis and on the extent to which databases are linked. (In many companies, for example, the databases that track ordering are completely separate from those that track fulfillment.) Privacy concerns can make it tough to acquire behavioral data, especially in business-to-consumer markets. Finally, database marketing to date has been used primarily as a tactical tool. A few striking counterexamples notwithstanding, its main goal has been to efficiently acquire customers, not to maximize customer asset value or to inform management of the total marketing system.

Companies that want to maximize customer equity need to expand their use of databases beyond acquisition marketing. Those that do not expand their focus, especially those that are highly acquisition oriented, may find themselves endlessly targeting and swapping promising-looking "switchers." They will not succeed in managing customer life cycles or in making sense of customer interactions, nor will they understand the trade-offs between acquisition and retention. On the other hand, companies that integrate databases into their relationship and customer valuation efforts as part of a broader customer equity approach will be able to balance acquisition programs with targeted, effective retention efforts and to capture greater customer asset value.

## Quantifying Customer Value

Customer equity management relies on the ability to measure and model customer value. This means delving beneath the surface of aggregate measures in order to assess the financial ramifications of strategies and tactics at the subsegment and individual levels. It also means measuring causal factors such as promotion frequency or customer satisfaction that drive changes in customer value.

Examples of metrics and accounting measures for customer equity are included in several of the subsequent chapters in this book. In addition, detailed examples of metrics are available at www.customerequity.com.

## Computing Customer Equity

To compute customer equity we need a mathematical equation that represents the specific relationships between key variables (e.g., retention rates) and customer equity and that allows us to model how the marketing mix can affect these key variables. The fundamental equation of customer equity (*CE*) is as follows:

$$CE(t) = \sum_{i=0}^{I} \left[ N_{i,t}\alpha_{i,t}(S_{i,t} - c_{i,t}) - N_{i,t}B_{i,a,t} + \sum_{k=1}^{\infty} N_{i,t}\alpha_{i,t}\left(\prod_{j=1}^{k}\rho_{j,t+k}\right) \right.$$

$$\left. (S_{i,t+k} - c_{i,t+k} - B_{i,r,t+k} - B_{i,AO,t+k})\left(\frac{1}{1+d}\right)^{k} \right]$$

$$CE(t) = \sum_{k=0}^{t} CE(t-k)$$

where

$CE(t)$ = the customer equity value for customers acquired at time $t$

$N_{i,t}$ = the number of potential customers at time $t$ for segment $i$

$\alpha_{i,t}$ = the acquisition probability at time $t$ for segment $i$

$\rho_{i,t}$ = the retention probability at time $t$ for a customer for segment $i$

$B_{i,a,t}$ = the marketing cost per prospect ($N$) for acquiring customers at time $t$ for segment $i$

$B_{i,r,t}$ = the marketing in time period $t$ for retained customers for segment $i$

$B_{i,AO,t}$ = the marketing costs in time period $t$ for add-on selling for segment $i$

$d$ = the discount rate

$S_{i,t}$ = sales of the product/services offered by the firm at time $t$ for segment $i$

$C_{i,t}$ = cost of goods at time $t$ for segment $i$

$I$ = the number of segments

$i$ = the segment designation

$t_o$ = the initial time period

This expression, which may seem somewhat messy to those no longer versed in mathematics, captures the crucial concepts of customer equity measurement. Let us translate. Customer equity equals

- the profit from first-time customers (which is the number of prospects contacted multiplied by the acquisition probability and the margin)

- minus the cost of acquiring the customers (which is the number of prospects multiplied by the acquisition cost per prospect)

- plus expected profits from future sales to these newly acquired customers (which is the retention rate in each future period multiplied by the profit obtained from customers in that period and then divided by the discount rate—which transforms future profits into current dollars, or any currency—summed across all future periods),

- summed across all customer segments and cohorts.

Simply put, a firm's total customer equity equals returns on acquisition plus returns on retention plus returns on add-on selling across a firm's entire customer portfolio over time. This means, then, that a company must identify the strategic balance that maximizes the sum, not any particular part. It includes determining the profit or loss that each strategy yields at different levels of investment and which strategy yields the highest return given a fixed investment.

Whether you delve into the details of this equation or not, the key point here is that a rigorous equation that defines customer value does exist, and that analysts and marketers can use it to choose actions that maximize the value of a company's customer assets.

In the chapters that follow, we show how to build up customer equity from acquisition equity, retention equity, and add-on selling equity. Our Web site, www.customerequity.com, provides specific examples of the computation as well as spreadsheets showing the steps in the process.

### Statistical Models to Relate the Marketing Mix to Customer Equity

Most books on customer relationship management make general pronouncements about how the firm can change retention rates, generally focusing on improving customer satisfaction. Marketing mix variables such as pricing are rarely linked to retention.

In reality, statistical models can be used to link marketing mix variables such as pricing and promotion to key parameters of the fundamental equation. A statistical tool called a *logit model* allows the analyst to link different price offers with the acquisition response rates resulting from those offers. (Logit models are discussed in more detail in chapter 4.) The firm can determine the mathematical relationship between acquisition price and acquisition response rate, and then optimize the acquisition price based on its effect on customer equity. Similarly, a company can model the retention rate as a function of retention pricing using statistical techniques and data relating retention pricing to retention rates. This in turn means it can determine the optimal retention pricing by segment based on the long-term value of the customer, not simply current sales.

Statistical modeling advances customer equity management well beyond the current state of gut feelings. The firm can determine how pricing, advertising, and channel decisions affect the long-term value of the customer. The fundamental equation and statistical and analytical models make these relationships clear and allow the firm to manage them to optimize acquisition, add-on selling, and retention spending and tactics.

### Case Study: Buford Electronics

To demonstrate how firms can use customer equity measurement, let's look at Buford Electronics. (The company name and data have been disguised.) Each year, Buford Electronics distributes $350 million worth of electronic components to a wide variety of customers throughout the United States. Its customers range from large corporations with many plants to small construction companies that order single parts for specific jobs. The company maintains distribution depots in approximately seventy-five major markets. Each depot has delivery services for its major customers and a pick-up counter where customers can come to collect their orders themselves.

Concerned that its smaller-volume customers represented little long-term value to the firm, Buford was considering a quantity discounting policy that would favor its larger-volume customers. By raising prices and then offering a quantity discount to larger customers, the thinking went, Buford would retain fewer—but presumably more profitable—customers. Before making such a change, however, Buford's management wanted to quantify its options. It decided to take a closer look at the profitability and long-term value of customers with whom it did less than $3,000 worth of business a year. Management compared these figures with the customer equity of Buford's higher-volume customers, with whom it did between $25,000 and $100,000 worth of business per year.

To conduct this analysis, Buford focused on customers who made their first purchases in 1995. For these customers, table 2-5 provides the estimated costs and profitability associated with acquisition. The table shows that the first-year ratio of dollar margin to selling expense for Buford's low-volume customers is significantly higher than it is for the firm's high-volume customers. In fact, this ratio is less than 100

**Table 2-5**
Customer Acquisition Financial Statistics

|  | *Low-Volume Customers* (Under $3,000 per year) | *High-Volume Customers* ($25,000–$100,000 per year) |
|---|---|---|
| | *Assumptions* | |
| Close rate per prospect | 15% | 5% |
| Costs per sales call | $20 | $100 |
| Number of calls per prospect | 2 | 9 |
| First-year sales per customer | $1,200 | $44,000 |
| First-year sales margin for a customer | $360 | $8,500 |
| Number of prospects targeted | 40,000 | 8,000 |
| | *Basic Financial Statistics* | |
| Selling costs per prospect | $40 | $900 |
| Cost to acquire a customer | $267 | $18,000 |
| Net profit (loss) to acquire a customer | $93 | ($9,500) |
| Ratio of first-year margin to selling expenses | 135% | 47% |
| Number of customers acquired | 6,000 | 400 |
| Initial customer acquisition investment | $1,600,000 | $7,200,000 |
| Acquisition equity (Net profit/loss of newly acquired customers) | $560,000 | ($3,800,000) |

percent for the high-volume customers. The first-year return from the high-volume customers is thus less than the initial selling costs associated with them. Acquisition equity, another important statistic contained in table 2-5, sums up the situation. *Acquisition equity* is the net profit or loss of acquisition for an entire customer group. Table 2-5 shows that the high-volume buyers have negative acquisition equity and that the low-volume buyers have positive acquisition equity.

This acquisition information, though very important, does not complete the picture. An assessment of *retention equity* is also necessary before one can make judgments about Buford's customer management strategy. Computing Buford's retention equity requires an understanding of how the two customer cohorts will behave in the future. Table 2-6 contains the historical purchasing behavior of these two groups since their first purchases. Using extrapolation techniques and the information in table 2-6, table 2-7 projects the behavior of these customers into the future. (Statistical models such as regression analysis can be used to predict future customer behavior based on the firm's marketing plan.) The firm now can determine the retention equity for each cohort based on the historical and projected statistics.

Finally, by combining the findings on retention and acquisition equity, table 2-8 computes the total customer equity for each customer class. As the table shows, the low-volume customer cohort has higher total customer equity and higher average equity per customer. Key reasons for this are the lower profit margins of the high-volume customers, which contribute to negative acquisition equity, and the lower retention rates of the high-volume customers. If the high-volume customers had greater retention rates, that could help Buford to recoup some of its loss on their acquisition. Alternatively, the firm could increase its high-volume customers' equity by becoming more efficient at acquisition. Buford could do this by increasing the prospect close rate, decreasing selling costs, or both.

When Buford's top management saw the computation of customer equity for the two customer groups, it realized that its low-volume customers represented significant long-term economic value, and that a pricing strategy that decreased their retention rate would hurt the company's overall customer equity. Buford management therefore decided against increasing base prices and offering steeper quantity discounts. A thorough understanding of customer equity prevented the company from pursuing a marketing strategy that would have proved a costly mistake.

**Table 2-6**
Average-Customer Performance Statistics

| Year | Sales ($) | Gross Margin (%) | Margin ($) | Marketing and Servicing Costs ($) | Retention Rate (%) |
|---|---|---|---|---|---|
| LOW-VOLUME CUSTOMERS: FIRST PURCHASE IN 1995 | | | | | |
| 1995 | 1,200 | 30.0 | 360 | 267 | |
| 1996 | 1,700 | 35.0 | 595 | 75 | 75.0 |
| 1997 | 2,300 | 35.0 | 805 | 75 | 80.0 |
| 1998 | 2,500 | 40.0 | 1,000 | 50 | 85.0 |
| 1999 | 2,500 | 40.0 | 1,000 | 50 | 85.0 |
| HIGH-VOLUME CUSTOMERS: FIRST PURCHASE IN 1995 | | | | | |
| 1995 | 44,000 | 19.0 | 8,500 | 18,000 | |
| 1996 | 52,000 | 24.0 | 12,480 | 1,000 | 40.0 |
| 1997 | 70,000 | 26.0 | 18,200 | 1,000 | 55.0 |
| 1998 | 85,000 | 27.0 | 22,950 | 400 | 65.0 |
| 1999 | 85,000 | 27.0 | 22,950 | 400 | 65.0 |

**Table 2-7**
Extrapolated Average-Customer Performance Statistics

| Year | Sales ($) | Gross Margin (%) | Margin ($) | Marketing and Servicing Costs ($) | Retention Rate (%) |
|---|---|---|---|---|---|
| LOW-VOLUME CUSTOMERS: FIRST PURCHASE IN 1995 | | | | | |
| 2000 | 2,500 | 40.0 | 1,000 | 50 | 85.0 |
| 2001 | 2,500 | 40.0 | 1,000 | 50 | 85.0 |
| 2002 | 2,500 | 40.0 | 1,000 | 50 | 85.0 |
| 2003 | 2,500 | 40.0 | 1,000 | 50 | 85.0 |
| 2004 | 2,500 | 40.0 | 1,000 | 50 | 85.0 |
| HIGH-VOLUME CUSTOMERS: FIRST PURCHASE IN 1995 | | | | | |
| 2000 | 65,000 | 27.0 | 17,550 | 400 | 65.0 |
| 2001 | 65,000 | 27.0 | 17,550 | 400 | 65.0 |
| 2002 | 65,000 | 27.0 | 17,550 | 400 | 65.0 |
| 2003 | 65,000 | 27.0 | 17,550 | 400 | 65.0 |
| 2004 | 65,000 | 27.0 | 17,550 | 400 | 65.0 |

**Table 2-8**
Total Customer Equity

### Low-Volume Customers: First Purchase in 1995

| | | | | | | | | |
|---|---|---|---|---|---|---|---|---|
| Number of Customers Acquired | | 6,000 | | Discount Rate | | | 20% | |
| Acquisition Equity | | $560,000 | | Total Customer Equity for Cohort | | | $9,586,823 | |
| Retention Equity | | $9,026,823 | | Average Customer Equity per Customer | | | $1,598 | |

| Year | Sales ($) | Gross Margin (%) | Margin ($) | Marketing and Servicing Costs ($) | Profit per Customer ($) | Discounted Profit per Customer ($) | Retention Rate (%) | Total Number of Customers during Year | Annual Total Discounted Profit for Cohort Group ($) |
|---|---|---|---|---|---|---|---|---|---|
| 1995 | 1,200 | 30 | 360 | 267 | 93 | 93 | — | 6,000 | 560,000 |
| 1996 | 1,700 | 35 | 595 | 75 | 520 | 433 | 75.00 | 4,500 | 1,950,000 |
| 1997 | 2,300 | 35 | 805 | 75 | 730 | 507 | 80.00 | 3,600 | 1,825,000 |
| 1998 | 2,500 | 40 | 1,000 | 50 | 950 | 550 | 85.00 | 3,060 | 1,682,292 |
| 1999 | 2,500 | 40 | 1,000 | 50 | 950 | 458 | 85.00 | 2,601 | 1,191,623 |
| 2000 | 2,500 | 40 | 1,000 | 50 | 950 | 382 | 85.00 | 2,211 | 844,066 |
| 2001 | 2,500 | 40 | 1,000 | 50 | 950 | 318 | 85.00 | 1,879 | 597,880 |
| 2002 | 2,500 | 40 | 1,000 | 50 | 950 | 265 | 85.00 | 1,597 | 423,499 |
| 2003 | 2,500 | 40 | 1,000 | 50 | 950 | 221 | 85.00 | 1,358 | 299,978 |
| 2004 | 2,500 | 40 | 1,000 | 50 | 950 | 184 | 85.00 | 1,154 | 212,485 |

(continued)

**Table 2-8 (continued)**
Total Customer Equity

### High-Volume Customers: First Purchase in 1995

| Number of Customers Acquired | 400 | Discount Rate | 20% |
|---|---|---|---|
| Acquisition Equity | -$3,800,000 | Total Customer Equity for Cohort | $388,108 |
| Retention Equity | $4,188,108 | Average Customer Equity per Customer | $970.27 |

| Year | Sales ($) | Gross Margin (%) | Margin ($) | Marketing and Servicing Costs ($) | Profit per Customer ($) | Discounted Profit per Customer ($) | Retention Rate (%) | Total Number of Customers during Year | Annual Total Discounted Profit for Cohort Group ($) |
|---|---|---|---|---|---|---|---|---|---|
| 1995 | 44,000 | 19 | 8,500 | 18,000 | -9,500 | -9,500 | — | 400 | -3,800,000 |
| 1996 | 52,000 | 24 | 12,480 | 1,000 | 11,480 | 9,567 | 40.00 | 160 | 1,530,667 |
| 1997 | 70,000 | 26 | 18,200 | 1,000 | 17,200 | 11,944 | 55.00 | 88 | 1,051,111 |
| 1998 | 85,000 | 27 | 22,950 | 400 | 22,550 | 13,050 | 65.00 | 57 | 746,447 |
| 1999 | 85,000 | 27 | 22,950 | 400 | 22,550 | 10,875 | 65.00 | 37 | 404,325 |
| 2000 | 85,000 | 27 | 22,950 | 400 | 22,550 | 9,062 | 65.00 | 24 | 219,010 |
| 2001 | 85,000 | 27 | 22,950 | 400 | 22,550 | 7,552 | 65.00 | 16 | 118,630 |
| 2002 | 85,000 | 27 | 22,950 | 400 | 22,550 | 6,293 | 65.00 | 10 | 64,258 |
| 2003 | 85,000 | 27 | 22,950 | 400 | 22,550 | 5,244 | 65.00 | 7 | 34,806 |
| 2004 | 85,000 | 27 | 22,950 | 400 | 22,550 | 4,370 | 65.00 | 4 | 18,853 |

## Optimizing Acquisition, Retention, and Add-on Selling

Customer equity management is built around three core strategies: acquisition, retention, and add-on selling. From the moment a company decides to target customer prospects to the time these customers make their final purchases, these strategies provide a framework for all marketing decisions. Every marketing activity affects an acquisition, retention, or add-on selling effort, or a combination of them.

These three strategies are not new to marketing, but the way in which customer equity management combines them is. Most companies apply them in isolation. They embark on acquisition drives with special promotions. They develop new customer service initiatives to improve retention. They come up with new product lines to increase revenues through add-on selling. But rarely do they investigate the links between these strategies or conduct the rigorous financial analyses necessary to show which strategy deserves the most investment at any particular time. A firm that uses customer equity management, on the other hand, understands each strategy in terms of both its effects on the other strategies and its contribution to total customer value over time. Chapter 7 includes a detailed discussion of strategies and tactics for optimizing the mix of acquisition, retention, and add-on selling.

Many early Internet marketers failed to recognize the concept of optimization. Rather than design customer acquisition programs matched to prospects' potential customer equity and linked to robust retention strategies, many firms blindly adopted a "first-in always wins" mentality and raced to acquire customers before the competition did, investing astronomical amounts for this purpose. Those schooled in customer equity know that acquiring more customers is not sufficient to overcome back-end profit levels or retention rates that are too low. eToys forgot about order fulfillment, causing great customer dissatisfaction and huge customer defection. MotherNature.com did not recognize it was easy for competitors to enter, and suffered from low retention rates. Pets.com spent $270 to acquire each customer in a 30 percent gross margin business. Could their customer retention equity level ever justify that level of investment in new customers?

### Retention Alone Is Not Enough

At this point you might ask, why not just focus on customer retention? After all, it has been well established that, on average, it costs far less to

retain a customer than to acquire a new one. This may not be the optimal strategy, however.

Consider aggressive promotional pricing programs used to acquire
customers. The lower the promoted price, the more "price shoppers"
the program acquires. This leads to lower retention rates, because these
price shoppers are more likely to defect when regular prices kick in.
Whether this is a good or a bad thing depends on each business's situation and strategic approach, but many companies benefit from acquiring more "triers" and then allowing those unwilling to pay the regular
price to defect. The key point here is that there is no universal pre-
scription. Only an assessment of acquisition, retention, and add-on selling equity values can determine which strategy makes sense.

Many existing approaches to retention marketing assume either
that all customers deserve a relationship approach or that only customers whose value justifies an investment in long-term relationship
building are worth serving. The former implies that the benefits of
relationship development always exceed their costs. This is not true.
Many firms should "fire" customers who have negative customer
equity, or raise fees to them. The latter assumption implies that only
the "best," most frequent-buying customers merit any sort of considered approach at all. But neither of these approaches applies univer-
sally. A balanced approach is more versatile and expands the set of tools
that companies can use to build customer equity.

In short, retention marketing, although useful, is incomplete. It
focuses on aggregate rather than individual customer requirements. It
is static, prescribing actions that do not change as customers move
through their life cycles. Finally, in the absence of precise measurement
of customer value, it cannot ensure that retention programs will pay for
themselves.

## Summary

The true worth of any business or marketing concept comes from its
ability to foster better decisions, generate higher profits, and increase
shareholder wealth. Customer equity meets these criteria, as well as the
standards for marketing system effectiveness listed in box 1-1, by building on the four cornerstones discussed in this chapter. In doing so, it
brings a discipline and rigor to the management of customer assets that
previously have only been applied to the management of portfolios of
tangible assets.

# PART II

# CUSTOMER STRATEGIES

# 3

# MANAGING
# CUSTOMER ACQUISITION

COMPANIES MUST ACQUIRE assets before they can manage them. For this reason alone, customer acquisition merits our attention. But customer acquisition is also important for other reasons. The most obvious is that all firms—even those with high retention rates—lose customers and thus must continuously acquire new customer assets. Second, the more efficient and effective a company's customer acquisition, the larger the pool of affordably acquired assets whose retention and add-on selling value can be captured.

Third, the customer–firm relationship developed during the acquisition stage strongly influences retention and add-on selling. Much depends on the kinds of customers a firm acquires and on the expectations that these customers have. Many firms behave as if the strategic elements of customer equity—acquisition, retention, and add-on selling—function independently. For example, firms often analyze data about existing customers without considering response and interaction data about nonacquired prospects. This results in misleading conclusions and missed opportunities because it gives no insight into what prevented the nonacquired prospects from becoming customers. Failing to link customer acquisition to retention also leads to other errors, including inaccurate forecasts about how long customers stay, the profitability of customers, and the impact of marketing efforts.[1] The usual result: a myopic, acquisition-fixated marketing strategy that leaves substantial customer equity on the table.

## What Is Customer Acquisition?

There are two ways to define customer acquisition. The acquisition *transaction* perspective says that customer acquisition ends with a customer's first purchase. The acquisition *process* perspective states that acquisition includes the first purchase as well as other nonpurchase encounters that both precede and follow the purchase, up until the time the customer makes a repeat purchase.

The process perspective is better because it includes the initial bonding and development stage of the customer–firm relationship. This is a very important time, during which the customer forms attitudes about the firm's product and ancillary services. It includes interactions such as customer service encounters that affect the customer's decision whether to purchase again. Managers, for their part, face many difficult business decisions at this stage, such as how much to invest in courting prospects and what service levels to offer them. Throughout the acquisition process, companies incur significant nonproduct costs. For instance, financial planners often meet with clients several times prior to first purchases, and direct marketers may send numerous mailings before prospects respond. Then, once a first purchase is made, a customer may request service or other activities that impose further costs. All this is part of customer acquisition. The retention phase of the relationship begins once the customer decides to make the first repeat purchase.

## Which Firms Should Emphasize Acquisition?

Although all firms need to direct some attention toward customer acquisition, the optimal amount of that effort depends on a business's ability to retain customers, its customers' repurchase frequency, and its relative opportunity to acquire versus retain customers.

Some industries simply have low retention rates. How many people, for example, go back to the same used car dealer to purchase a car? Used car sales has long been an acquisition business. Businesses whose products have low purchase frequencies also favor an acquisition-heavy approach. Consumer durable-goods firms focus on acquisition in response to the fact that many of their products have ten-year to fifteen-year lives, and in recognition that many uncontrollable factors affect retention rates for products with such long purchase cycles.

At the other extreme are firms with exceptionally high retention rates due to high switching costs. These rates raise the future equity of acquired customers. Switching banks, for example, can entail significant costs for individual customers and business clients alike. Once customers make a commitment, they want to stay put. As a result, banks can and should focus a larger share of their effort and expenditures on acquisition.[2]

Firms in new or underdeveloped markets should direct a higher percentage of their marketing investments toward customer acquisition, in order to generate awareness and penetration for their products. Internet-based companies frequently forsake short-term profits to build a customer base.[3]

## Developing a Customer Acquisition Strategy

### Selective Acquisition

Historically, the pursuit of market share has driven the customer acquisition investment of the majority of companies. The attitude has been to acquire as many customers as possible, as AOL did in 1997 when it acquired 500,000 new customers in one month.[4]

Fewer firms have adopted *selective customer acquisition* policies. This approach assumes that not every potential customer is worth the customer acquisition investment. For example, credit card companies use risk-based prospect management, which assesses a prospect's credit risk prior to a credit card solicitation. Based on this assessment, the company decides whether to pursue the prospect, and makes an offer appropriate to the prospect's risk level.

Computer manufacturers such as Dell and Compaq also employ selective customer acquisition strategies based on their marketing channel models. Dell relies on a direct-sales system with no intermediaries and limited pre- and postpurchase service. (Examples of prepurchase service include providing information about product attributes, assembling the machine once purchased, and providing training that helps novices understand how to use the software.) In contrast, Compaq has used higher-service retailers to distribute its product. As a result, Dell is more likely to attract experienced buyers, who need less sales and service support, whereas Compaq's service offerings are more likely to attract beginners. The lesson here: Channel choice has substantial customer equity implications.

Although potentially more difficult to manage, the selective customer acquisition approach creates customer equity. Because the profiles of the acquired customers are more likely to match the firm's ideal target market, retention rates and add-on buying rates are likely to be higher. These benefits are especially critical to firms for which (a) it often costs more to acquire a customer than to retain one, and (b) the majority of the potential customer base is not very profitable.

### Customer Acquisition Rules

Four rules help companies to optimize acquisition.

> *Rule 1: Acquire any customer as long as the discounted future value of the customer exceeds the acquisition costs for that customer.*

A firm should continue to invest until it no longer can cover its investment on the last incremental customer. Most firms apply this rule's logic to capital investment strategy but not to customer investment strategy. Instead of investing in customer acquisition until the net present value (NPV) of the marginal customer falls to zero, the typical firm will underinvest, stopping with prospects whose NPV is far greater than zero. By underinvesting, the firm fails to maximize its customer equity. Rule 1 can be difficult to put into practice because many firms do not know what it costs to acquire individual customers. These firms set initial acquisition budgets with little regard for future customer value; or worse, set overall marketing budgets without linking expenditures to acquisition, retention, and add-on selling goals.

> *Rule 2: When you broaden the acquisition effort, be prepared for lower response rates.*

This is the corollary to rule 1, and assumes that firms target their best customers first, their second-best customers second, and so on. Given this process, a firm faces diminishing response rates as it tries to acquire more customers. Following rule 1 without recognizing this principle of diminishing returns will lead to significant overspending on acquisition. A typical acquisition curve looks like figure 3-1.

> *Rule 3: The greater its profits from retention, the greater a firm's customer acquisition investment should be.*

**Figure 3-1** Acquisition Curve: Incremental Response Rate

This may seem counterintuitive: Why should high retention profits lead us to focus more strongly on acquisition? It can be shown mathematically that the greater its retention rate or the higher its add-on selling potential, the more a firm can invest in future customers. The logic is simple: If future profits from a customer are high, then the firm can afford to lose more on its initial investment to acquire the customer. The firm therefore can increase its acquisition effort, acquiring more customers whose retention and add-on selling value can be captured.

*Rule 4: The higher the percentage of the initial acquisition investment that a firm recovers in the first period, the greater its acquisition investment should be.*

Early returns determine the risk level of the investment. Assuming the same economic return, why not choose a lower risk? Although a discount rate can be used to adjust for risk, most managers prefer faster payoff investments because of the uncertainty of the future.

Rules 3 and 4 lead to the four acquisition strategies shown in figure 3-2 and described in the following list.

- *Full Throttle:* High retention-profit potential combined with short-term investment recovery makes new customer acquisition a major opportunity. The firm invests as much as possible in acquisition until the NPV of the marginal customer is negative. The risk of this strategy is low, and its return is high.

*Customer Equity*

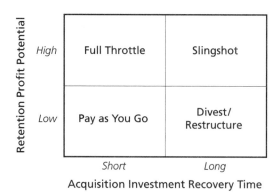

**Figure 3-2**  Acquisition Investment Strategy Matrix

- *Slingshot:* High retention-profit potential combined with a long investment recovery time calls for a slingshot strategy, so named because the more invested in acquisition, the greater the future payout. The long time until payout—initial investment is very high relative to first-year returns—makes the investment risky. The firm must bet on a high NPV driven by high retention profits. A slingshot strategy is typical of the customer-investment environment among Internet companies. Many e-tailers invested heavily in acquisition spending without recognizing the risk associated with lower-than-expected retention profits.

- *Pay As You Go:* This strategy is most appropriate when retention-profit potential is low and acquisition-investment recovery time is short. (Most of the investment recovery occurs during the first period.) The firm invests as though all profits will accrue in the current period. Short-term profit goals drive the firm's investment.

- *Divest/Restructure:* In this situation, a firm must restructure its marketing system. Customer acquisition will not pay out because the initial payback is low *and* retention and add-on sales are low. The firm will not be profitable in the long run, and it will have very low customer equity.

## Targeting: The American Express (U.K.) Membership Rewards Program

The American Express Membership Rewards program provides points to American Express Cardmembers for money they spend using the card. These points can be used to buy products and services such as airline tickets, sporting equipment, and electronics. When the Rewards program attempts to acquire new customers it has an enormous asset at its disposal: intimate details of its target market. Only Cardmembers can join the Rewards program, so the target market is clearly defined and very well known. American Express maintains detailed records on its Cardmembers, keeping track of their financial status and spending habits.

In 1996, the U.K. Rewards program had 1.5 million customers. It had achieved a 35 percent penetration rate of the overall Cardmember base. However, that penetration level had peaked, and acquisition efforts were beginning to deliver diminishing returns. Attrition was increasing because members who had received their first year free were now being asked to pay a £20 membership fee. The Rewards managers decided that they needed to embark on a new acquisition strategy, based on two approaches: profiling of existing customers to identify the characteristics of high-potential prospects, and research on nonacquired prospects to determine whether different acquisition products or approaches were needed.

To use existing customer profiling, they built a model that predicted two things. First, the model predicted which Cardmembers were most likely to agree to become Rewards members by looking at characteristics of the existing members and correlating these characteristics with those of the Cardmembers who were not yet Rewards members. Second, the model predicted which cardholders would also increase their use of the card if they became Rewards members. Those Cardmembers who fit both profiles became the targets of a telemarketing effort. In particular, the model segmented Cardmembers into deciles, analysis of which led to several conclusions:

- Acquiring prospects from the first three deciles would be the most profitable because they were the most likely to convert and to increase use of the card.

- Members from the next three deciles (4 through 6) would allow reasonable profitability.

- The program would break even or lose money over the life cycles of members from the members of the remainder of the deciles.

Based on the model, the team focused its marketing efforts on the first six deciles and did not invest in trying to convert the others.

In the second initiative, focus groups from among nonacquired prospects (American Express Cardmembers who were not also Rewards members) uncovered the following information:

- Although in general the prospects thought that the program was good, they felt it was not for them because its focus was on travel.

- They did not want to pay a membership fee.

- They found the rewards to be distant because too many points were required to qualify for awards.

Based on these data, the team concluded that the Rewards program in its current state would never attract these customers.

To change this, program managers did the following:

- Targeted more local partners for the reward program. The local partnerships—restaurants, theaters, and other retail establishments—would increase the accessibility of benefits, particularly for those who seldom traveled.

- Devised a tiered program, adding a new tier to the program that had no annual fee but paid out award points at a lower rate per pound spent. The new program, Rewards Essential, both served as an acquisition product for customers who could later trade up to the original program, and, with its lower cost to American Express, matched the cost of the Rewards program with the customer equity value of the acquired customers.

Both initiatives led to increases in customer equity for both American Express and the Rewards program. The Rewards program successfully segmented its market and developed separate products for each segment. In addition, the program carefully targeted only those members of the segment who would most enhance customer equity if they decided to join—that is, the members who were likely to (and had the financial wherewithal to) increase their overall card usage the most.

## Customer Acquisition Tactics: The ACTMAN Model

Targeting, the most common focus of acquisition tactics, is only one part of managing acquisition. In this section we outline a model called ACTMAN, an acronym for *acquisition tactical management*. The ACTMAN model distills the acquisition process into six critical elements that a firm can manage for more efficient and effective customer acquisition. These elements are as follows:

1. Targeting

2. Awareness generation and product positioning

3. Acquisition pricing

4. Trial

5. Usage experience and satisfaction

6. Postintroductory pricing and the creation of long-term value for the product or service

Figure 3-3 illustrates the ACTMAN model, which is described briefly in the following subsections. A more detailed description of the model and its application, including example calculations, is available online at www.customerequity.com.

### *Targeting*

A firm should target both those customers who recognize that they have a need or desire for the firm's offerings as well as those who have not yet identified their needs or desires but who could benefit from the firm's offerings. This latter group may be more difficult to acquire because the firm will have to aid their need recognition using vehicles such as suggestive advertising or sampling.

Three methods exist for targeting customers: individual-customer targeting (first-degree targeting); segmented targeting (second-degree targeting); and self-selection targeting (third-degree targeting), which relies on the customer to identify himself or herself by responding to the firm's offers. First-degree targeting is the most desirable, but in some industries it is difficult to employ cost-effectively.

#### FIRST-DEGREE TARGETING
The two commonly used first-degree targeting methods are profiling and regression scoring. Both methods depend on the availability of demographic, behavioral, or psychographic data on potential customers that a company then matches with prospects' likelihood to buy or with their potential customer equity value. Once the characteristics of high-value prospects have been identified, the most attractive prospective customers can then be targeted and solicited.

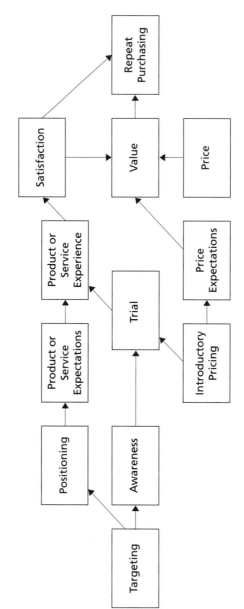

**Figure 3-3** The ACTMAN Model

## SECOND-DEGREE TARGETING

Second-degree targeting utilizes segment data rather than individual data, and should be used when individual customer or prospect data are unavailable.

Sometimes a firm can classify prospects and customers into segments for which data (often readily available governmental data) already exist. Many consumer-product firms, for example, develop lifestyle clusters based on geodemographic census tract data from the U.S. Census Bureau. They then analyze these clusters to determine which best match current customer profiles.

Second-degree targeting, like first-degree targeting, uses statistical models. An example: General Seed, a direct marketer of floral seeds, had demographic data for each U.S. zip code. It also knew the number of mailings and the response rate (the number of customers acquired each year) for each zip code. Using standard regression techniques, the model predicted the zip code response rates as a function of demographic and climatological variables. The firm then determined the economic cutoff level above which a zip code—that is, all the people in it—should receive a mailing.

## THIRD-DEGREE TARGETING

Even when customer data are not available at either the individual or segment level, a firm can use targeting techniques. In these cases, targeting must be accomplished through marketing programs. This is called self-selection or third-degree targeting.

In self-selection targeting, a firm makes a marketing offer, such as introductory pricing or a promotional incentive, designed to cause certain desirable types of customers to respond. For this approach to succeed, a firm must be able to determine whether a specific promotion, price, or product can attract the desired prospects. The channel chosen to convey the offer will also affect who responds.

## TARGETING SUMMARY

The most efficient targeting method is individual scoring, which allows a firm to select customers to be targeted based on their economic payout to the firm. Segment-based models are less efficient, but are better than nondatabase (self-selection) targeting methods as long as the predictive power of the models is strong enough to differentiate between segments.

Whenever possible, companies should do their targeting at the level of individual customers. If in doubt, do a quick calculation of the cost of more-focused solicitation versus the customer equity value of customers missed and gained as a result—you'll likely be convinced.

### *Awareness Generation and Positioning*

Once a firm has identified its target customers, it must make sure that they are aware of its product or service. After all, a prospect cannot try a product until he or she knows it exists. There are many tactics a firm can use to generate awareness. Direct marketing communication can combine awareness generation with product offers for trial, and is the method of choice when first-degree targeting is used. Mass communication is a less expensive mechanism for generating broad awareness in second- and third-degree targeting environments, or where the value of an acquired customer is relatively low. For example, many Internet companies use mass communications (television, radio, billboards, print) to generate awareness and to invite customers to log on to their Web sites to learn more about products and services. These companies have learned that awareness generation through direct communications, even through portals and other Web services such as AOL, tends to push acquisition costs too high. Instead, these companies use lower-cost vehicles for awareness generation and more targeted communications for customers once they have responded. This is where positioning comes in.

According to Philip Kotler, "Positioning is the act of designing the company's offering and image so that they occupy a meaningful and distinct competitive position in the target customers' minds."[5] Positioning is critical to new customer development because it defines customer expectations about the product experience, and it determines whether customers will try a product or not.

In order for a product or service to be included in the customer consideration set, the firm must manage the critical steps of proper awareness building and positioning while the customers are in the information-gathering stage of their purchase decision-making process. Firms also need to remember that if positioning and awareness-generation efforts promise too much, then customers may try the product, but retention rates will fall short as a result of customer dissatisfaction. A firm must carefully balance its initial positioning against the product's ability to deliver the promised benefits, or risk destroying the potential customer equity from retention and add-on selling. Acquisition is an important part of marketing, but not the only part—linkages across acquisition, retention, and add-on selling are crucial for companies that want to maximize customer equity.

### Acquisition Pricing

As customers accumulate product information and begin to evaluate their alternatives, pricing becomes a factor. The general trend in customer-oriented pricing is to price low to acquire customers and to raise prices later. This tactic, known as *penetration pricing*, works in many situations. The biggest challenge for a firm that chooses penetration pricing lies in determining the most effective introductory price level. Guidelines exist on how to set introductory prices under various circumstances, assuming that a firm can tailor its prices by customer segment.[6]

For example, introductory prices should decline as a segment's maximum retention potential goes up. As a corollary, the more responsive a group is to retention marketing expenditures, the lower its introductory price should be. Introductory prices should be higher for groups that become more price sensitive over time, because a firm ultimately will have to lower prices to retain them as customers. The higher introductory price will compensate for this future decrease in revenue. (Among the customers who fall into this category are those who typically buy only on promotion.) Higher introductory prices also make sense for many evolving markets, in which more purchase options will likely become available, leading to increased customer price sensitivity over time.

A special category of customer acquisition is reacquisition of lapsed or lost customers. In this instance, it is almost always possible to use existing purchase data to estimate customer asset value with confidence. As a result, firms can set "winback" prices that are below those offered to other acquisition targets in recognition of the high asset value of the reacquired customers. Companies should be cautious, though: It is very easy to get into a reacquisition war, as long-distance telephony providers did when they used teaser rates and other price-based promotions to acquire switching-prone customers from each other, over and over again, at tremendous cost. The flaw, of course, was in incorrect assumptions about how long reacquired customers would stay, and the risk of "re-loss."

### Retention Pricing

It may seem strange that retention pricing is a consideration of acquisition management. However, if one recalls that customer acquisition is a process that continues beyond the actual purchase, and that postpurchase behavior is the final stage of the customer purchase-decision model, then the relevance of retention pricing to acquisition becomes clear. In order for customers to leave the acquisition phase and move into the repeat-purchase phase of the customer life cycle, they must reach an acceptable level of satisfaction with the product experience, and expectations about future experiences must be attractive. Assessing the attractiveness of future experiences involves some consideration of future pricing.

Acquisition pricing can greatly influence expectations about retention pricing. The acquisition price acts as a reference price for customers in their assessment of future prices. If the retention price is too high relative to this reference price, customers are less likely to repurchase the product or service. As a result, pricing strategy must include how a firm will manage the change in price between acquisition and retention. If a very low acquisition price attracts prospects who would not otherwise try the product, then charging a significantly higher retention price will cost the firm a large number of first-time buyers. That does not necessarily invalidate this strategy, but a firm must understand the complete financial implications of this pricing strategy and the fact that the quality of the product may not suffice in keeping these types of customers on board. In general, firms should avoid acquisition pricing tactics that create price expectations that retention pricing cannot meet.

One way to manage reference prices is to use special promotions that signal one-time price discounts off regular prices. Another way is to list long-run prices along with the special introductory prices in price communications. The danger remains, however, that once a price goes up from the low introductory price, the customer will not feel that the product provides a value above his or her threshold.

### Trial

Many firms identify product trial as a key strategic objective. It marks the point at which customers move from evaluating alternatives to actually making purchases, and it is often the first signal of interest that customers communicate to the firm. From a firm's perspective, the goal of the trial stage, besides generating revenue, is to demonstrate to customers that the firm's product or service can meet their needs.

Firms commonly use price discounts or free offers as mechanisms to induce trial. Although such tactics may prove successful at initiating a first usage, it is important to manage them carefully, both because customer expectations still are being established during the trial stage and because at the time of first usage, the customer may not have committed to repurchasing the product. If product expectations are very high as a result of initial selling communications, and if the product fails to meet these expectations, the customer probably will not repeat-purchase, and the lifetime value of that customer will likely be low or even negative.

It is at this stage that product strategy begins to play a role in customer equity creation. Companies should manage their product portfolios to include acquisition products—those that are appealing to customers early in their buying life cycles. Sloan's brand ladder at GM from Chevrolet to Cadillac is one example; other examples of acquisition products include demand deposit accounts at banks and books at Amazon.com.

### Usage Experience and Satisfaction

In addition to marketing communications, which play a key role in establishing customer expectations, two other critical activities significantly influence the customer's product usage experience and satisfaction:

- Product design and the provision of specified benefits

- Postpurchase servicing of the customer

The firm's ability to meet expectations depends on its research and development team, which manages product or service design; its operational staff, which controls production and delivery; and its customer service team, which manages postpurchase servicing. It is important that each of these teams be aware of its role in customer management and the development of customer equity. If any one of these areas of the firm does not deliver on its responsibilities, the customer is unlikely to be satisfied. Even if the product or service is clearly superior to any other on the market, if expectations go unfulfilled, then the customer will be disappointed and less likely to repeat-purchase.

## The U.S. Armed Forces and Acquisition

For the U.S. Armed Forces (Army, Navy, Air Force, Coast Guard, and Marines), the job of acquiring "customers"—the men and women who enlist for active duty—has become increasingly challenging over the past few years. Because of the robust economy and absence of a compelling, specific military mission such as defeating communism, fewer young people are choosing to enlist in the military. Yet, to survive at its current size, the military must recruit 200,000 new members each year.

To replace (recruit, train, and equip) an Armed Forces' member who leaves prematurely costs taxpayers more than $35,000. Given the high replacement cost, military recruiters concluded that the retention potential of a recruit is a substantial consideration in their acquisition strategy.

Although the Armed Forces is a somewhat atypical "customer" setting, many ACTMAN elements still apply.

### *Targeting*

According to the Department of Defense, marketing research and experience indicate that the most successful recruits—those who are best able to adapt to military life and become long-term service people—are high school graduates who score at or above the fiftieth percentile of the Armed Forces Qualification Test.

Currently, 93 percent of the active duty enlisted personnel (not including officers) are high school graduates with no college degrees (figure 3-4). Based on these findings, along with the age limit and physical requirements, the Armed Forces identified their first-tier targets as people aged seventeen to twenty-four years who are soon-to-be or recent high school graduates.

### *Awareness Generation*

Given the increased options for their potential recruits, the Armed Forces have initiated aggressive campaigns to increase awareness among its target audience. Campaign efforts include billboard advertisements, direct mailing, and cold calls to identified candidates.

The Air Force launched a $28 million ad campaign that is being broadcast on movie screens and during prime time programs such as *Monday Night Football*, NBA games, and television dramas popular with the targeted age group, such as *Buffy the Vampire Slayer* and *Dawson's*

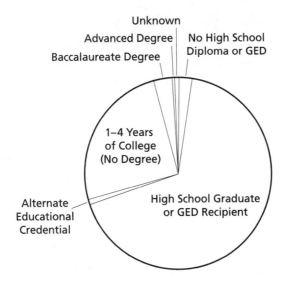

**Figure 3-4** Education Level of Active-Duty Military (Enlisted)

*Creek.* As a joint recruitment effort, the Armed Services created eight new television ads, with spots on ESPN, MTV, TNN, and other stations frequently viewed by young adults. The new ads utilized MTV-style special effects, with live-action footage shot at various U.S. military installations.

Recruiting offices are also on the move, away from downtown storefronts and into malls with high youth foot traffic. And "acquisition pricing" is being used, with inducements such as double signing bonuses and shorter mandatory commitments being offered to spur enlistment of members of the targeted prospect audience.

### Trial

In selected high schools throughout the country, students are able to participate in the Junior Reserve Officer Training Corps (JROTC). JROTC is a set of noncompulsory high school classes that teach military principles. Service men and women teach these classes. Student participants are required to go through simulated basic training, wear uniforms, and are given military-like ranks. Based on their experience, some JROTC students sign up for active duty after graduation, whereas others attend college on ROTC scholarships. Scholarship winners promise to serve in active duty after graduation. Participants in the JROTC are able to exit the program, without consequences, at any time.

### *Usage Experience and Satisfaction*

For the military, as with companies, meeting "customer" expectations is important to retention and thus key to the acquisition process. The branches of the Armed Forces are designed with several customer service and operational divisions in order to facilitate the transition to military life and increase personnel satisfaction. These divisions handle issues ranging from day care to career counseling to religious concerns. Personnel satisfaction is high in areas such as career opportunities (including tuition reimbursement) and benefits (travel, medical, and housing). Finally, in most cases the military is able to satisfactorily meet and manage expectations because of its clear guidelines.

In the last ten years each branch of the Armed Forces has had a difficult time meeting recruitment numbers. However, in 2000 the Department of Defense reported that enlistment is increasing among its target group. In fact, by mid-2000, the Air Force had already met its recruitment target and others were expected to follow.

## Methods and Tools for Acquisition

In this and the following chapters on retention, add-on selling, and optimizing the customer equity strategy, we will provide brief descriptions of the tools and tactics that companies can use. In each chapter, we discuss

- Databases and data sources

- Metrics and accounting

- Data analysis tools

A detailed examination of these areas is beyond the scope of this book and its intended audience; however, detailed descriptions, including formulas, example calculations, and data displays, are available online at www.customerequity.com.

### *Databases and Data Sources for Acquisition*

#### Prospect Databases

Prospects are not customers, and the firm needs to use different marketing tactics to affect their behavior. Therefore, companies should separate prospect databases from customer databases. Prospect data fall into two categories: historical marketing data and profile data.

Historical marketing data track marketing activity by individual prospect. These data include the prospect source, each marketing con-

**Table 3-1**
Example of Historical Marketing Data for Prospects

| Data Element | Internal/External Source | Source |
|---|---|---|
| Prospect source | Internal | Marketing |
| Marketing contacts | Internal | Sales force |
| Promotional offers | Internal | Marketing |
| Stage of sales cycle | Internal | Sales force |

tact, and the response to each marketing contact. Table 3-1 gives examples of recommended historical marketing data.

CUSTOMER PROFILE DATABASES
Profiling customers (or prospects) is the process of obtaining detailed information about them. This information can range from demographic data (such as family size) to personal data (such as hobbies). The results of profiling help a firm to determine the best messages to convey, products to target, and communications to avoid. They can reduce costs by helping a firm to target new or existing customers for add-on selling more efficiently. In short, they are an important part of customer equity management.

There are six main categories of profile data:

1. Customer sales potential

2. Customer characteristics (such as demographic, lifestyle, and industry classification data)

3. Summary customer equity measures

4. Organizational charts and key personnel (business-to-business)

5. Influencers and specifiers

6. Customer attitudes

Table 3-2 lists types of profile data with their sources.

Sales potential is one of the most valuable elements of the customer or prospect profile. This data element includes the customer's potential sales volume, not just actual purchases. Analysts compute potential in different ways, depending on the market under consideration. For example, credit card companies often use information about outstanding balances from all the credit cards of a cardholder. (They obtain

**Table 3-2**

Example of Customer (or Prospect) Profile Data

| Data Element | Internal/External Source | Source |
|---|---|---|
| Customer sales potential | External/Internal | Third party data, sales force, marketing research |
| Customer characteristics | External/Internal | Third party data, sales force, marketing research |
| Customer equity | Internal | Accounting, marketing research |
| Organization structure | Internal | Sales force, marketing research |
| Key influencers | Internal | Sales force, marketing research |
| Specifiers | Internal | Sales force, marketing research |
| Competitors' products used | External/Internal | Sales force, marketing research |
| Customer's attitudes | External | Marketing research |

these data from credit bureaus.) This information provides insight into the customer's profit potential. Industrial or business-to-business firms often use firm size and industry type as surrogates for sales potential. Firms can obtain estimates of customer potential from industry trade associations or third parties.

A profile database also must contain demographic data. For consumer products, these data usually also include lifestyle information. Industrial firms typically include firm size and industry classification in their demographic data. They may also include personal information about customers, organizational charts, and other pertinent details.

Attitudinal data are important because they indicate how a customer evaluates the firm. For example, retained customers (such as airline passengers) may nonetheless have negative attitudes about the products or services that they use. These vulnerable customers are more likely to defect, so firms need to take steps to affect their attitudes. Databases that contain attitudinal data help firms to identify these customers and to design marketing programs aimed at affecting their attitudes. Historically, few firms tracked attitudinal data because of the cost and difficulty of collecting such data. However, with the advent of the Internet, the cost of customer surveys has declined and will continue to do so.

## Causal Marketing Databases

Causal marketing databases capture data on the marketing programs offered to individual prospects and customers. They are extremely complex to create, because firms rarely track marketing activities at the individual-customer level. However, they are also extremely valuable, because the information they contain can significantly improve marketing efficiency and effectiveness. By knowing the cost of and responses to various marketing activities, companies can determine which pay out and which are unprofitable.

For example, companies can use targeting models developed from causal data to identify which customers should receive specific marketing communications. Years ago, Time Life Books sent mailings for a book series to its entire customer base. The company then realized that it could target its mailings, which greatly reduced overall mailing costs without significantly reducing overall response. To do this, Time Life developed sophisticated targeting models. It sent sample mailings to the customer base, tracked marketing offers and responses by customer, and then scored customers according to their responses. In subsequent mailings, Time Life targeted those customers whose scores indicated they were likely buyers.

A business-to-business firm applied a similar approach. It tracked all sales-force activity and found that it should greatly reduce direct sales calls on a large set of its prospect and customer base because the expected revenue from these customers could not cover the cost of the calls. The firm put in place a sophisticated two-tiered marketing system, which substituted phone calls for a large number of the sales calls. The company found that response did not drop; in many circumstances the customer actually preferred the phone call to an hour spent with a salesperson.

Table 3-3 lists recommended elements of a causal marketing database. To track these data, companies need the ability to match marketing activities to customers (or prospects, as the case may be), and in many cases must have disciplined sales forces that are willing to complete sales call reports. Firms unwilling to commit to tracking information about marketing activities are at a disadvantage. Savvier firms recognize that investments in these efforts pay off in improved efficiency.

**Table 3-3**
Example of Causal Data

| Data Element | Internal/External Source | Source |
|---|---|---|
| Sales calls per customer or prospect | Internal | Sales force call reports |
| Product or service offers | Internal | Marketing |
| Pricing to customer | Internal | Accounting |
| Promotional offers | Internal | Marketing |

## *Measuring and Accounting for Acquisition*

A simple way of thinking about customer equity is that it is the sum of acquisition equity (the value of the customer up to the point of repeat purchase), retention equity, and add-on selling equity. This chapter discusses acquisition equity.

### Computing Acquisition Equity

Computing acquisition equity is usually straightforward (the difficulty arises in obtaining the data to make the computations), and consists of six steps:

1. Determine the number of prospects contacted over a fixed time period from a completed acquisition campaign.

2. Measure the marketing and servicing costs associated with contacting and selling to the prospects.

3. Determine the number of prospects who became customers.

4. Compute the sales revenue and gross margin for the new customers' first set of purchases.

5. Compute the acquisition equity of the entire pool of customers by subtracting the costs calculated in step 2 from the revenues calculated in step 4. Note that this equity number can be negative.

6. Divide the total acquisition equity by the number of customers to determine the average acquisition equity per customer.

Computing acquisition equity sets the stage for using customer equity data in a company's accounting system.

## ACQUISITION METRICS

Top management is often surprised by the high cost of customer acquisition. How can companies determine what acquisition expenditures make sense? Basic knowledge of acquisition costs, initial profit-to-cost ratios, and new-customer investment statistics provides management with a better understanding. As these measures become more widely used, firms can benchmark against other firms in similar industries. Ultimately, these and other customer equity metrics can, and we believe should, become part of firms' financial reporting as companies truly begin to manage customers as they manage other valuable financial assets.

Critical summary statistics for acquisition include the following:

- Number of customers acquired, which can be tracked over time and matched to a company's acquisition goals.

- Acquisition rate, which is the ratio of acquired customers to targeted prospects. This statistic measures both targeting and solicitation effectiveness. It can be broken down further to assess success rates with different groups of prospects.

- Cost of acquiring a customer, which can be matched to customers' retention and add-on selling values, and which also influences how aggressively companies should expand their acquisition expenses.

- Total new-customer investment, which allows a company to compare its investment in creating customer assets with its investments in capital equipment, product development, and research.

- The ratio of acquisition cost to acquisition equity, which shows how much of its acquisition investment a company recovers in the first period. High-recovery situations, as noted earlier, reduce the risk of increased spending on customer acquisition.

- Total new-customer investment as a percentage of sales and profits. These percentages are critical measures because they show whether a firm is investing in new-customer acquisition at the same level as in prior periods or simply is milking existing customers for profitability.

Another critical measure is the net present value of a new customer. Once acquired, a new customer has a future value, which equals the sum of all future purchases minus the cost of goods sold and future marketing expenses. Firms must understand the future value of acquired customers so that they can determine whether investing in new customers is profitable. If it is not profitable, the firm must change its acquisition approach.

To increase total customer equity when the NPV per customer declines, it is necessary to increase, not decrease, the investment in new customers. There is a limit to this increased investment, however. The per-customer acquisition cost must not exceed the marginal NPV for the "last" customer acquired. As long as the firm acquires customers with NPVs greater than acquisition costs, the firm should be willing to increase its customer acquisition investment. Otherwise, the long-term value of its customer base will decline.

### *Data Analysis Tools for Acquisition*

In this and subsequent chapters, we provide brief summaries of analysis tools for converting customer data into insights for acquisition, retention, and add-on selling.

Customer-focused data can be used, among other things, to do the following:

- Identify target customer segments

- Determine customer acquisition rates

- Determine customer retention and defection rates

- Identify opportunities for add-on selling

- Understand and evaluate consumer responsiveness to marketing programs

- Track and analyze customer buying patterns

- Measure the economic value of the customer

- Forecast and manage future customer behavior

- Develop more effective customer-focused strategies

In this section, we present two techniques that can be used to target new customers for acquisition: profiling and regression scoring. A comparison of the strengths and weaknesses of each of these techniques is shown in table 3-4.

**Table 3-4**
Customer Acquisition Data Analysis Tools

| Customer Acquisition Analysis Technique | What It Demonstrates | Advantages | Disadvantages |
| --- | --- | --- | --- |
| "Best customer" profiling | Characteristics of most profitable customers | Simple and easy to understand<br><br>Almost any firm can use some form of profiling, if it has a database | Depends on the firm's targeting strategy<br><br>Has blind spots—only looks at characteristics of today's customers |
| Profiling using indexing | Over- and underrepresentations of customer types in acquired customer set | Provides a comparison between the general population of a product's consumers and the firm's existing customers for that product<br><br>Identifies characteristics of acquired customers | Slightly more complex than profiling<br><br>Could overlook segments that have higher targeting potential<br><br>Does not identify causal drivers of customer acquisition |
| Regression scoring | Drivers of acquisition value | Provides a scientific method for selecting cutoff values<br><br>Measures the relative importance of variables in determining which prospects to target | More complicated than profiling; could require outside resources |

PROFILING

The simplest way to determine how to target new customers is to profile existing ones. In profiling, a firm identifies the characteristics of its
best current customers and then targets noncustomers with similar
characteristics. These "noncustomers" can be first-time purchasers
from the firm or individuals who have purchased from other divisions
of the firm.

*An Example of Profiling.* To identify prospects for acquisition targeting,
an analgesics retailer began by obtaining demographic data at the
individual-customer level. The company compared heavy users and
category purchasers with noncustomer users. Table 3-5 shows the distribution of its customers across various demographic variables; the
first column reflects the percentage of the general population represented by that demographic type (drawn from government statistics
and prior marketing studies).

The second column, the profiling index, represents the fraction of
the firm's customers that fit into that demographic type relative to the
total number of potential analgesic customers in the general population. An index of 100 is average; less than 100 means that the firm has
fewer than the average number of customers who match that demographic category. With these data, the retailer now can target nonbuy-
ers who fit the profile with mailings, coupons, and samples.

Business-to-business marketers can use the same targeting technique. (The profiling data likely will come from sources, such as Dun &
Bradstreet, that are different from those tapped by consumer companies.)

*How to Profile.* A relatively simple form of profiling is "best customer"
profiling. Steps include the following:

1. Collect demographic and profitability information about current
   customers.

2. Append this information to each customer's record in a profiling
   database.

3. Add behavioral data (such as sales histories) and psychographic
   data to each profile.

4. Determine which variables distinguish the best customers, worst
   customers, and nonresponders.

5. Use these variables to identify the highest-potential prospects.

**Table 3-5**
Example of Profiling: Analgesics

| Demographic Variable | Percentage of General Population | Profiling Index |
|---|---|---|
| Household size (HH): 1 member | 25 | 71 |
| HH size: 2 members | 33 | 117 |
| HH size: 3–4 members | 31 | 103 |
| HH size: 5+ members | 11 | 105 |
| Female HH head age: <35 | 19 | 74 |
| Female HH head age: 35–44 | 19 | 97 |
| Female HH head age: 45–54 | 18 | 115 |
| Female HH head age: 55+ | 26 | 131 |
| Female HH head age: No female HH head | 18 | 69 |
| HH income: <$20K | 23 | 96 |
| HH income: $20–29.9K | 20 | 102 |
| HH income: $30–39.9K | 14 | 95 |
| HH income: $40–49.9K | 12 | 98 |
| HH income: $50–69.9K | 18 | 102 |
| HH income: $70K+ | 13 | 108 |
| Female HH head educ: Not HS grad | 6 | 128 |
| Female HH head educ: HS grad | 33 | 120 |
| Female HH head educ: Some college | 27 | 101 |
| Female HH head educ: College grad | 17 | 84 |
| Female HH head educ: No female HH head | 18 | 69 |
| HH head occupation: Professional | 28 | 89 |
| HH head occupation: White collar | 11 | 89 |
| HH head occupation: Blue collar | 28 | 100 |
| HH head occupation: Not in work force | 32 | 114 |

Indexing, another form of profiling, compares the general population of a product's consumers with the firm's existing customers for that product. To index:

1. Partition customers in the database using several demographic variables.

2. Determine the number of buyers that fall into each partition.[7] The index for each partition reflects the ratio of the number of

the firm's customers in that partition to the total number of the buyers in the general population that fit that partition.

In its simplest form, this index shows for which demographic categories a firm has more than the expected number of customers and for which it has fewer. Those partitions that have significantly higher indices indicate customer segments that the firm has effectively targeted and acquired. Partitions with lower indices represent those segments that the firm acquires less effectively.

*Advantages and Disadvantages of Profiling.* Almost any firm that has a customer database can easily profile. However, when profiling, analysts must remember that the firm's targeting strategy can influence the characteristics of its customer base. Put another way, it should not be surprising when a company that has been targeting a specific audience finds, through profiling, that its customers come from that audience. As a result, the firm's profiling risks overlooking other valuable segments of potential customers.

Analysts should also interpret profiling indices with caution. Some segments may have high targeting potential but not appear frequently in the database; therefore, profiling will not identify them as attractive targets. Also, a firm should assess the potential customer equity of each partition before using a profiling technique to target new customers. A segment with a low index may actually be a very high asset value segment that the firm's acquisition strategy underemphasizes. Finally, profiling does not include the statistical analyses needed to assess the strength of various characteristics as predictors. It tells analysts the characteristics of the firm's best customers, but not which characteristics are the most powerful identifiers of potential "best" customers.

## REGRESSION SCORING

Companies can also use regression scoring, a more difficult but more accurate technique than profiling, to target new customers.

*An Example of Regression Scoring.* Contract Stationers, Inc. (a disguised example) sells office supplies to businesses. Because making sales calls on every prospect costs too much, management decided to target specific prospects instead. The firm obtained a targeted prospect list of

**Table 3-6**
Weights and Scores for Selected Prospects

| Customer Number | Unweighted Values | | | | Weighted Values | | | | |
|---|---|---|---|---|---|---|---|---|---|
| | Constant | Firm Size (000) | No. of Employees | Service Sector | Constant | Firm Size (000) | No. of Employees | Service Sector | Score |
| Weight | — | 1 | — | — | 7 | 0.0017 | 0.054 | 3.1 | — |
| 1 | 1 | 2,438 | 153 | 0 | 7 | 4.1446 | 8.262 | 0 | 19.41 |
| 2 | 1 | 99 | 8 | 1 | 7 | 0.1683 | 0.432 | 3.1 | 10.70 |
| 3 | 1 | 208 | 27 | 0 | 7 | 0.3536 | 1.458 | 0 | 8.81 |
| 4 | 1 | 679 | 38 | 1 | 7 | 1.1543 | 2.052 | 3.1 | 13.31 |
| 5 | 1 | 1,431 | 45 | 0 | 7 | 2.4327 | 2.43 | 0 | 11.86 |
| 6 | 1 | 541 | 58 | 1 | 7 | 0.9197 | 3.132 | 3.1 | 14.15 |
| 7 | 1 | 65 | 7 | 0 | 7 | 0.1105 | 0.378 | 0 | 7.49 |
| 8 | 1 | 987 | 103 | 1 | 7 | 1.6779 | 5.562 | 3.1 | 17.34 |
| 9 | 1 | 2,431 | 305 | 1 | 7 | 4.1327 | 16.47 | 3.1 | 30.70 |
| 10 | 1 | 354 | 31 | 0 | 7 | 0.6018 | 1.674 | 0 | 9.28 |

firm names and individuals from various publications and list sources, such as Dun & Bradstreet.

Using these data, the firm made a series of sales calls on a randomly selected set of prospects and then noted who responded, added customer characteristic data to each prospect's record, and ran a scoring model to determine which characteristics generated the highest likelihood of response. The resulting variables and weights appear in table 3-6, along with the scores computed for ten prospects.

The firm aggregated the prospects' scores into decile groups. (Scores also can be grouped into smaller sets, such as 5 percent groupings, if researchers prefer.) The firm then calculated the likelihood of purchasing for each decile group. Table 3-7 shows a typical decile table, with score ranges and buying probabilities.

The firm determined the cutoff score by computing a break-even customer equity value, which was based on buying probabilities, marketing costs, and long-term expected sales to the customers.

By using regression scoring, this firm improved its acquisition efficiency and avoided sales calls on prospects with negative long-term value. It targeted only customers whose projected customer equity was positive and thereby increased its total customer equity by a substantial amount.

**Table 3-7**
Decile Ranges and Probability of Response

| Decile Number | Score Range | Number of Prospects | Percentage Responding |
|---|---|---|---|
| 10 | >25.47 | 493 | 31.33 |
| 9 | 20.39–25.47 | 493 | 27.42 |
| 8 | 18.61–20.38 | 493 | 21.47 |
| 7 | 15.18–18.60 | 493 | 18.36 |
| 6 | 13.43–14.99 | 493 | 15.89 |
| 5 | 12.87–13.42 | 493 | 14.11 |
| 4 | 11.47–12.86 | 493 | 12.79 |
| 3 | 10.51–11.46 | 493 | 9.30 |
| 2 | 8.31–10.50 | 493 | 6.41 |
| 1 | <8.30 | 493 | 4.68 |

*How to Perform Scoring.* As suggested by the example, regression scoring steps include the following:

1. Draw a random sample from the overall population of prospective customers.

2. Obtain data from the sample that profile individual consumer characteristics.

3. Initiate a marketing campaign directed at the random sample, and record which individuals become customers.

4. With that information, develop a regression scoring model—a series of weighted variables that predicts which prospects are more likely to become customers based on their characteristics.

Once researchers have the model estimates, they can do the following:

- Calculate scores for prospects who were not in the random sample by plugging their individual characteristics into the regression equation

- Rank-order prospects from highest to lowest, according to their scores

- Target the firm's marketing campaign at those prospects with scores above a designated cutoff score, which is based on a combination of financial and marketing factors

*Advantages and Disadvantages of Regression Scoring.* The primary advantages of using regression scoring models for acquisition are that they measure the relative importance of variables in determining which prospects to target, and they provide a scientific method for selecting cutoff values. The result is significantly increased marketing efficiency.

The primary disadvantage of regression scoring is its complexity relative to profiling. However, we recommend that firms seriously investigate implementing regression scoring, even if it requires using outside resources. Improved targeting efficiency and effectiveness usually justify the increased complexity and costs.

## Summary

Managing acquisition strategies and tactics is vital to creating, sustaining, and enhancing customer equity. Acquisition should not be viewed as a secondary element in a customer equity marketing system, even in the most retention-oriented industries. Similarly, traditional marketing strategies that fail to consider acquisition's links to retention and add-on selling are also deeply flawed. As the ACTMAN model shows us, all elements of the acquisition process—from the creation of customer expectations to postpurchase customer service—have long-term implications for the customer–firm relationship. A retention-focused firm that neglects its acquisition strategy will never maximize retention and add-on selling. By the same token, any acquisition strategy that fails to consider its long-term effects on retention and add-on selling is incomplete.

# 4

# Managing
# Customer Retention

THE TOP MANAGEMENT of a major Midwest grocery retailer met in Traverse City, Michigan, in July 2000 to evaluate the information gathered through the company's frequent-shopper card program. The initial presentation by the marketing director included some astounding information: 30 percent of the company's customers represented over 75 percent of its profits. But like many other retailers, this grocery chain focused its marketing activities on driving traffic into the stores by using hot promotions and loss leaders. The president and COO warned the assembled group, "We're in a new era of retail marketing. We must begin to understand and manage our key customers much better than we have in the past. The future of the firm rests on our ability to retain our customers. Competitors like Wal-Mart are making major inroads into our customer base. It is no longer enough to bring customers in with our weekly ads; we must learn how to provide a unique environment for our top customers."

At the next meeting, the COO brought in all 150 of his store managers. On the wall of the meeting room hung 1,500 pictures organized by store number. The COO asked each store manager to look at the pictures from his or her store and to identify the people in them. Almost no one could. The COO then explained that for each store there were 10 pictures, one for each of the store's top ten customers. The COO went on to tell the store managers that they had better begin to learn not only who those top ten were, but also who the top fifty were—and by name.

This story may seem extreme, but it is not. Most companies have just begun to recognize the power of customer retention. Small changes in retention rates can significantly affect a firm's total customer equity. A quick example: If a company increases its annual retention rate from 75 percent to 80 percent, it increases a customer's expected lifetime from four years to five years. In other words, a 6.67 percent improvement in the retention rate increases the customer's expected lifetime by 25 percent. This simple analysis suggests why so many business books are focused on retention.

Before proceeding, one note of caution is in order. Many popular approaches to retention marketing have a fatal flaw: They assume that changes in retention rates come at no cost. Nothing could be further from the truth. It is extremely difficult to change a company's retention rate from 75 percent to 80 percent. Changing retention rates without significantly rethinking many of an organization's fundamental systems, processes, and even culture may be almost impossible.

## Defining Customer Retention

Retention, like acquisition, is not simple to define. One possible definition of customer retention is the following: The customer continues to purchase the product or service over a specified time period. Unfortunately, not all products are purchased frequently enough to make this definition applicable to many high-valued, low-frequency-of-purchase products. In the brokerage industry, for example, a customer who does not buy a security within a fixed time period (e.g., a quarter or year) may nonetheless intend to buy when the conditions are right.

This leads to an alternative definition:

- *For products with short purchase cycles:* The customer continues to purchase the product or service over a specified time period.

- *For products with long purchase cycles:* The customer indicates the intention to purchase the product or service at the next purchase occasion.

This definition, of course, raises the question of how to define long-purchase-cycle products. To match the typical financial reporting period for a firm, it simplifies retention analysis to define long-purchase-cycle products as those with purchase cycles longer than one year.

In some businesses, a customer's intentions cannot be determined from financial outlays. For example, some online magazines such as Salon.com do not charge people to read them. However, frequent and regular readers may be considered retained customers because they signal the company through their behavior that they intend to continue their relationship with the firm. Therefore, the definition of retention must not assume that revenue from a customer determines whether or not the customer is retained.

Attrition and silent attrition are also important terms. *Attrition* (defection) occurs when the customer has decided to no longer use the product or service and has communicated to the firm that he or she is no longer a customer. However, most customers do not communicate to the firm that they have defected. *Silent attrition* occurs when the customer has decided to no longer purchase the product or service but has not indicated to the firm that he or she is no longer a customer. In most business settings, silent attrition poses serious problems because managers cannot identify when a customer is no longer a customer. This makes it very difficult to determine if a customer is retained.

One final note: Retention is not the same as loyalty or "share of requirements." A customer who invests some money through a traditional brokerage and some through an Internet brokerage may not be considered loyal to either, but this customer is retained by both. In short, retained customers do not need to be loyal.

## Myths about Customer Retention

Customer retention can be critical to a firm's success, but it is not a magic bullet. Before we discuss customer retention strategies and tactics, it is important to debunk two myths:

1. A firm should strive for 100 percent customer retention.

2. Maximizing customer retention is synonymous with maximizing a firm's profits.

The idea that a firm's maximum retention rate is not 100 percent (or at least some fixed number close to that) may seem counterintuitive. However, factors both within the firm's control (e.g., price) and beyond it (e.g., customers' desire for newness) affect its customer retention potential, making the assumption of a maximum 100 percent retention rate incorrect.

Consider the airline industry. It makes sense that airlines strive for 100 percent retention among their top customers. These customers have exceptionally high lifetime value. However, aiming for similar retention rates among very price conscious college students would be foolish. Airlines use yield management pricing techniques to put these customers on the plane for as little as 10 percent of the prices they charge their best, frequent-flying customers. But airlines recognize that college students are not loyal—they seek the lowest fares—and generally do not have high retention rates because after college many move to other markets with different hub airlines.

So, should the airlines avoid adding these low-valued, price-sensitive fliers who are incrementally profitable? Obviously not. If an airline concentrated on and compensated its managers on overall retention rate alone, it would not serve this customer segment. By accepting a retention rate of less than 100 percent, the airline can gain customer classes who have lower inherent retention rates but add incremental profits. The bottom line: It makes sense to treat some customers as "transaction" customers, not relationship ones.

It is also critical to understand that maximizing customer retention is not synonymous with maximizing a firm's profits. You might guess that it is optimal for an airline to retain 100 percent of its best, frequent-flying customers. This would be true if maximum attainable retention ensured maximum profits. But it does not, and here's why. An easy way to increase retention rates is to offer lower prices to the best customers. If an airline charges this group too little, it leaves money on the table. It is better off losing some high-valued customers at the expense of its retention rate, because the profits gained by charging higher prices to the majority who are retained exceed the profits lost from the defectors. The result is an optimal retention rate among high-valued customers of less than 100 percent. This optimal rate depends on the price sensitivity of the best customers and their inherent retention rate.

The key lessons are as follows:

- The goal of customer retention management is *not* to strive for zero defections. Instead, a firm should manage its retention rate and choose retention strategies and tactics that best support its main focus: optimizing customer equity.

- Customer retention does not occur without incurring some costs. Companies can maximize customer equity by matching those costs to the retention values of individual customers rather than by acting on the myopic view that "retention is free."

## Determinants of Customer Retention

Many managers assume that customer satisfaction is the main determinant of customer retention. In this section, we cite empirical evidence that calls this assumption into doubt, and present an alternative model of the key factors affecting retention rates.

### *The Customer Satisfaction Trap*

Firms often seek to manage customer retention by managing customer satisfaction. In particular, they focus on achieving a certain level of satisfaction among *all* customers. Although this has some merit, these firms can easily become victims of a customer satisfaction trap: They increase customer satisfaction, yet reap none of the benefits—such as increased sales, profitability, or customer loyalty—supposedly associated with higher customer satisfaction levels.

A recent study focused on 20 companies that scored well in the 1988 and 1989 Baldrige competition. This study found that although customer satisfaction increased in these firms, customer retention levels either remained unchanged or declined.[1] A study of the auto industry revealed that although 90 percent of the industry's customers reported satisfaction with their purchases, repurchase rates were only around 30 percent to 40 percent.[2] A third study polled over 200 large American corporations and discovered that more than 90 percent of them had ongoing processes for measuring and improving customer satisfaction. However, only 2 percent of them could show increases in sales or profits resulting from their increases in customer satisfaction.[3] Some research has shown a correlation between satisfaction and retention.[4] However, the studies noted here suggest that customer satisfaction may not be the primary driver or cause of customer retention.

### *An Alternative Model of Customer Retention*

The customer retention process actually begins during acquisition, which creates customer expectations, including perceptions of product value and uniqueness. Initial product usage determines whether these expectations are met. Then other factors, such as ease of exit, ease of purchase, and customer service, come into play. Together these factors affect long-term customer behavior and determine the relationship between seller and buyer. Types of relationships are as follows:

- The highly loyal, committed customer
- The customer who is willing to continue purchasing the product or service, but who is vulnerable to competitive offers
- The defector, who abandons the product

In this model, there are seven determinants of customer retention:

1. Customer expectations versus the delivered quality of the product or service
2. Value
3. Product uniqueness and suitability
4. Loyalty mechanisms
5. Ease of purchase
   - Availability
   - Convenience
6. Customer service
7. Ease of exit (lock-out provisions)

The following subsections briefly explain how each variable affects customer retention.

### Customer Expectations versus Delivered Quality

Customers do not simply evaluate a product or service on its own merits. They evaluate it relative to their expectations. This is a crucial issue, because through its market communications a firm sets customer expectations. When customer expectations are too high (though this can generate initial trial) and the delivered product does not meet those expectations, the customer will not repeat-purchase. Thus a critical factor in determining retention is the *difference* between the customer's expectations and the delivered quality of the product or service.

Raising expectation levels generates trial, but overly high expectations contribute to low retention. A firm must strike the optimal balance between expectations and delivered quality.

VALUE

Here, we define value as quality divided by price. A firm can provide greater value either by offering higher quality and matching the competition on price or by offering the same quality at a lower price. Unfortunately, firms often try to justify higher prices by arguing that they provide greater quality. But quality is difficult to define and measure. From a customer equity perspective, firms should trade off the potential price premium against the risk of customer defection—and the resulting loss of substantial retention equity.

PRODUCT UNIQUENESS AND SUITABILITY

The more different (or less substitutable) a product is, the greater the retention rate. When a customer has access to almost identical products or services, the probability of purchasing any particular one decreases significantly.

In addition, it is critical that products remain relevant to customers. Just as the use of "acquisition products" is important in obtaining new customer assets, so too companies should ensure that their product portfolios contain "retention" offerings that customers can trade up to as they proceed through their life cycles.

LOYALTY MECHANISMS

Loyalty mechanisms can generate high retention rates even when competing products or services are almost identical. The airlines have used frequent-flyer programs to generate high degrees of loyalty even though their services are very similar. Retailers now use frequent-shopper cards or credit cards to induce customer loyalty. Neiman-Marcus has its In Circle card, which offers special services to its better customers. Target, a mass discounter, entices customers to use its credit card by donating 1 percent of their purchases to education. Such loyalty mechanisms, which link usage and rewards, can become very powerful generators of retention.

EASE OF PURCHASE

Some products and services are very difficult to find or purchase, which hurts retention. For example, a customer will not regularly buy a specialty brand of stocking if it is not widely available, even if the product is highly differentiated.

Ease of purchase is not only a consideration for retail companies; manufacturers of specialty industrial components also need to make sure that their products are easily available to buyers. W.W. Grainger addresses this problem by widely distributing specialty suppliers' products to the construction industry. Aeroquip, a maker of specialty hoses and fittings, invested in retail stores because it found that customers needed its products quickly. Because of the emergency nature of fixing a broken hose, if their customers could not obtain Aeroquip's brand within a short time period, they changed brands.

## CUSTOMER SERVICE

Clearly, customer service is an important factor in customer retention. In some recent studies, customer service was the most important determinant of whether or not a customer would defect from a firm. But defining customer service is not as easy for a company to do as it may seem.

Customer service has many components, and many parts of an organization provide it. Accounting provides customer service when it solves a customer's billing problems, logistics handles customer service problems when the product is not delivered, and engineering provides customer service when it shows a customer how to utilize the equipment more efficiently or how to increase production-line speed through a minor product modification. Customer service opportunities are pervasive in any organization.

The issue becomes how best to manage the process. No simple answer exists. Some companies have customer service representatives who are responsible for handling all customer problems. Other companies decentralize the process. For the customer equity–oriented manager, evaluating the range of service options comes down to three questions:

- What customers will this service approach retain, and for how long?

- What is the potential asset value of those customers?

- Does the retention equity created exceed the service cost?

## EASE OF EXIT

Exit barriers offer one strategy for increasing retention. Examples of these barriers include programs that reward continued use based on historical usage; product-design characteristics that make it difficult to

**Table 4-1**
Linkages to Customer Retention

| Factor | Relationship to Customer Retention |
|---|---|
| MARKETING TACTICS OR PROGRAMS | |
| Customer satisfaction | Evidence exists in both directions |
| Add-on selling | Positively related |
| Rewards or free gifts | Positively related |
| Services | Positively related (assuming they meet customer needs) |
| PRODUCT CATEGORIES | |
| Experiential products (products that are difficult to evaluate prior to use, e.g., legal services, cable television) | Higher levels of retention |
| Products with high switching costs (e.g., banks) | Higher levels of retention |

*Note:* Relationships noted in this table are supported by the empirical studies referenced in the text.

change suppliers; and product-learning curves that make it costly to switch to competing products.

EMPIRICAL EVIDENCE

What is the importance of each customer retention factor? Table 4-1 summarizes research about drivers of retention.[5–8] As shown, add-on selling (which increases the number of customer–seller interactions and linkages) and the use of rewards, gifts, and free services have been shown to increase retention levels. Products with high switching costs tend to promote retention, as do experiential products, because it is difficult to evaluate a service prior to its first use and costly to change it afterward.[9] As noted earlier, the evidence regarding the power of increased aggregated levels of customer satisfaction is mixed.

## Customer Retention at Amazon.com

Amazon.com acquired 11 million new customers in 1999, nearly tripling its number of customers (figure 4-1). One business analyst estimated in mid-2000 that the net present value of the ten-year earnings Amazon will generate from its current and future customers will

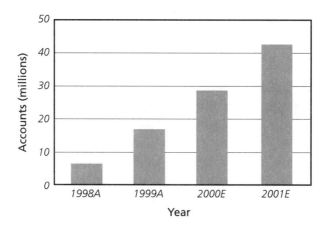

**Figure 4-1**  Cumulative Customer Accounts, Amazon.com
*Source:* Company reports and Deutsche Banc Alex. Brown estimates.

approach $50 billion (as compared with a market capitalization of $18 billion at the time this book was written).[10] Yet Amazon's greatest success in 1999 was not customer acquisition, but customer retention. Repeat customers accounted for 71 percent of Amazon's sales, up from 63 percent in the previous year.

As Amazon's customer base continues to increase, that base becomes an even more attractive target market. In 2000, 8 percent of U.S. households could be counted among Amazon's customers. Analysts estimate that by 2001, repeat-customer orders will account for 84 percent of Amazon's sales (figure 4-2).

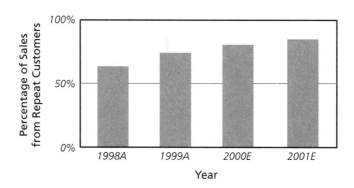

**Figure 4-2**  Repeat-Customer Orders for Amazon.com
*Source:* Company reports and Deutsche Banc Alex. Brown estimates.

How does Amazon achieve its enviable 78 percent retention rate and high level of sales to these retained customers? The answer lies in the company's strategy of creating a virtuous cycle:

1. Amazon endeavors to learn about its customers and their needs.

2. It uses this knowledge to offer value-added features to its customers.

3. These features, when used by its customers, add to Amazon's knowledge of these customers and increase the connections between them and the company.

4. This additional customer knowledge keeps the cycle going, allowing Amazon to create new product and service offerings.

Features such as Amazon's 1-Click ordering, Wish List, and recommendations create a personalized, convenient experience for customers and drive repeat visits and purchases. At present, an average active customer increases his or her spending with Amazon at a rate of 15 percent per year.

So what is Amazon's retention strategy? And how does it match up with our determinants of customer retention?

### *Loyalty Mechanisms*

We said that customer retention initiatives should start during the acquisition process; Amazon's does. During the initial purchase, Amazon collects data such as delivery address, credit card number, and item titles, which are analyzed to produce leverage for future purchasing. For example, if a customer logged on to Amazon.com to purchase *The Innovator's Dilemma* by Clayton Christensen, that customer would be presented with a number of pieces of information: the title's rank among books purchased from Amazon, average customer ratings by those who had purchased it, reviews written about the book by other Amazon customers (Amazon provides a $50 gift certificate to whomever writes the first review of a particular book), as well as with what groups this choice was popular. Additionally, several books would be recommended based on similar subject matter, such as *The New New Thing* by Michael Lewis and *Blown to Bits* by Philip Evans and Thomas Wurster. To complete the interaction, the customer is given the opportunity to rate the usefulness of the reviews of the book. So, even at the first transaction, Amazon is both adding value to the experience and beginning to tie the customer into the community of Amazon customers. These interactions produce a personal stake in the process, which promotes loyalty and return visits.

Similarly, the Wish List feature gives customers the ability to create online communities of friends and family to share gift lists and recommend books, CDs, and other items. As the name suggests, a customer can use this feature to create a list of items that he or she would like to purchase from Amazon. This list can then be forwarded to a group of people designated by the originator. Customers are able to search for the Wish Lists of others by name, address, and other distinguishable features. Customers can also use the Wish List simply to keep track of items for their own purchase at a later date.

### Ease of Purchase

While downtime and slow speeds are frequent complaints about Web sites, Amazon does provide greater convenience than most bricks-and-mortar stores. Through its Amazon Anywhere initiative, Amazon has struck deals that enable its customers to connect from their cell phones and personal digital assistants (PDAs), such as the Palm VII. Adding further to the company's ubiquity is the Associates program. Companies and individuals with Web sites can create links to Amazon's site and earn referral fees and bonuses by having visitors click from their site to Amazon.com to purchase items. In the second quarter of 2000, referrals accounted for 1.25 million, or about half, of the company's new customers. Analysts estimate that the company has a 26 percent annual referral rate.

The 1-Click feature stores customer information (such as the preferred shipping method, payment method, and shipping address) so that on future visits customers are able to place orders quickly, without having to enter this information again. This is coupled with a safe shopping guarantee, which assures that customers pay nothing if unauthorized charges are made to their credit cards.

### Customer Service

The company has also benefited from its reputation for having a well-trained and courteous customer service group that can be contacted by customers twenty-four hours a day via a toll-free number or e-mail. From the moment an order is placed, Amazon is in touch with the customer, beginning with a "thank you" confirmation e-mail. The e-mail includes a confirmation number, delivery date, other recommended books, and a link to track the order. Another key to Amazon's strong customer service reputation is its responsiveness. If a customer orders multiple items, one of which is currently unavailable, Amazon immediately e-mails the customer and gives him or her the option of receiving those items that are available now and the other at a later date at no additional cost.

### Customer Expectations versus Delivered Quality

Amazon also receives high marks for its fulfillment of customer expectations. In a recent customer (dis)satisfaction competition held by eConvergent, consumers were asked to submit both good and bad experiences with e-businesses during the 1999 Christmas season. One winner submitted the following story about Amazon: "This year I decided to shop online for my nephew's Christmas present. I chose Amazon.com over many of the other toy and retail sites because their site has a user-friendly reputation. Instantly I received an email confirming my order and the guarantee that the order would be delivered within two days. Just as promised, on my doorstep two days later was the order. The best part was that the gift was a hit and the overall experience took less than 15 minutes. I really had a great e-experience!" This customer typifies what many customers say about Amazon: The company delivers exactly what it says it will, in itself a surprising result.

### Product Substitutability and Suitability, Value, and Ease of Exit

Although Amazon lists more than 18 million items in categories including books, CDs, toys, electronics, videos, DVDs, home improvement products, software, and video games, its customers could find similar products elsewhere. Although Amazon's retention record is enviable, it is less clear whether its broad set of product categories will be relevant to its users over time. And, although it has comparable prices, it does not offer its products at a cheaper price than other retailers do. Finally, many of Amazon's customers are very adept online users who also use other sites. In the absence of clear product-line or price differentiation, Amazon must depend on its strength in the other relationship-building dimensions to build barriers to exit for its customers.

Most business readers have heard a lot about Amazon. Many stories have exalted the company, and just as many seem to be questioning whether the company can ever earn profits that would justify its high market value. In either case, Amazon is a good example of how to employ a customer retention strategy. Amazon begins the retention process as it acquires a new customer. It also works with these new customers to increase their purchases and refer other new customers. Most remarkably, Amazon achieves high retention and loyalty despite its lack of product or price differentiation.

## Customer Retention Strategy

This section discusses the dynamics of customer retention and the ways that retention, acquisition, and add-on selling strategies affect each other.

### *Changing Retention Rates*

Retention rates can be changed by increasing spending on retention programs or by improving the effectiveness of current retention programs. Figure 4-3 shows the relationship between the two approaches. If a firm wants to attain a certain retention level, it can either move along the lower curve by spending more, or it can shift that curve higher by implementing some type of management-process change. The latter approach increases retention without increasing current spending. Unfortunately, this is very difficult to do; although it may be the preferable option, it is not always feasible.

We can compare the two approaches by looking at how a company might make changes in customer service representation. The firm could decide to empower its customer service representatives, allowing

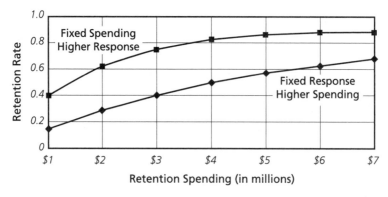

**Figure 4-3**   Comparison of Retention Spending Strategies

them to make rapid decisions in response to customer problems. This kind of change could increase retention rates without increasing costs. But if the company were willing to increase its retention spending, it could decide instead to add customer service representatives to its staff, which also would make it possible to respond to customer complaints and problems more quickly.

Both approaches are useful and commonly applied. Improving retention programs has the advantage of being a one-time investment, but a firm can have trouble identifying the necessary changes. Increasing spending can help a firm to attain its optimal retention-spending rate, but it carries the risk of inefficient overspending.

### *The Acquisition–Retention Link*

Just as expectations set during acquisition affect retention, so do customer retention strategies have implications for acquisition. Take the example of a health club that uses a low introductory price to attract new members, many of whom are very price sensitive and likely to defect if the membership price increases in the future. If renewal prices are kept low, the club would retain the low-value members, but risk losing high-value customers who are willing to pay more but dislike crowding and therefore go elsewhere. In this case, the best retention strategy may be to use a high membership renewal price to encourage the extremely price-sensitive customers—who are unlikely to be profitable—to defect.[11] This strategy makes sense if the customer equity being lost now from defecting high-value customers, plus the increased revenue from the higher renewal rates paid by those who choose to stay, exceeds the equity value that would be lost from nonrenewing low-valued customers. In all likelihood, the club manager will want to go even farther and recast her customer acquisition strategy to target, solicit, and acquire fewer, but higher-potential, customers.

The point here—that customer acquisition and retention strategies must be aligned—seems intuitive. However, if you polled 100 firms across various industries, very few of them would know—or if they did know, few would give much thought to—the tactics they use to acquire a customer or how those tactics affect customer retention. Instead of seeking to understand the relationship between acquisition and retention, many firms simply focus on managing customer satisfaction. And as we pointed out earlier in this chapter, research shows that may do little to improve retention—or customer equity.

### Short-Term Losses for Long-Term Gains

A firm may not want to retain all its customers, but the retention of desirable customers is an important goal. Studies indicate that consumers who remain with a firm longer tend to generate higher revenues per customer (because of add-on selling or increased purchases), cost less to serve, pay price premiums more willingly, and are advocates of the firm to other potential customers.[12] As a result, it may be in the firm's best interest to make suboptimal profits in the short run in order to nurture the customer–firm relationship and maximize customer equity over the total customer life cycle.

To successfully align acquisition, retention, and add-on selling strategies and to identify when it is appropriate to settle for suboptimal profits, managers should develop an in-depth understanding of customer behavior, characteristics, and likely responses to firm tactics. In addition to recency, frequency, and monetary value data on past purchases, managers should look at the following:[13]

- How buying patterns change over time
- How much customers purchase in a product category
- What customers purchase in complementary categories
- How customers respond to various promotions
- The level of customers' disposable income (for consumer markets)

This information captures a more holistic view of the customer–firm relationship than simple data on purchase levels and can better predict customer behavior. A firm will need a sophisticated customer database or data warehouse to develop this type of customer profile. Later in this chapter, we discuss these databases and the tools used to analyze their data.

### Retention Spending

The statement that by increasing retention spending a firm can increase retention rates and profitability is only partially true. As with other investments, expenditures on retention reach a point of diminishing returns.[14] Exceeding this level may lead to very small increases in retention but decrease the firm's customer equity. Given this possibility, firms need to understand when to increase or decrease their retention expenditures.

Research shows that when the retention margin potential of a customer or a customer segment increases, the retention expenditures directed at that segment should increase.[15] This finding makes intuitive sense. It seems less intuitively clear, but is nonetheless true, that when customers are very responsive to retention expenditures, a firm should spend less. A firm can afford to spend less on very responsive target customers because it takes less attention—in this case in the form of expenditures—to retain them. The same is true for a firm's maximum retention potential. Research shows that if the overall defection rate is already low, then a firm's retention expenditures should decrease.

### How Should a Firm Price Its Best Customers?

Pricing to top customers is a controversial and important issue in managing customer retention. The answer depends on a number of factors, the two most crucial of which are the following:

- Whether customer price sensitivity increases or decreases as a function of the number of purchases made

- The extent of word of mouth among customers

If price sensitivity decreases as the number of a customer's purchases increases, then the firm should increase the price to this customer over time. In general, a firm's best customers are less price sensitive because of their greater preference for the product, because they have become "locked in" over time to using the product, or because they do not search for alternatives. Whatever the reason, the firm should raise its price to these customers.

This concept contradicts most customer retention literature, because it means that a firm intentionally will lose some customers as a result of its pricing strategy. Although most firms believe that their best customers should be charged less, they often charge them more. The reason for this is simple: New customers often get discounts for trying a product, which makes their prices lower than the current list price. A firm rarely lowers prices for existing customers, who thus end up paying more than the newest customers do. Ironically, this is an excellent pricing strategy in most situations.

The exception to this rule is when there is substantial word of mouth among customers. In cases in which pricing and promotion data are widely known (as in many industrial markets, and increasingly in consumer markets with the penetration of the Internet), firms may be forced to charge best customers the lowest prices or risk losing them.

## Methods and Tools for Retention

### *Databases and Data Sources for Retention*

To manage the retention process, a firm needs to understand what influences repeat-purchasing decisions. Expectations, actual experience, perceived value, and satisfaction are some of the key elements that affect repeat purchasing. However, there is not much empirical evidence that indicates the causal factors that drive retention. As a result, retention databases benefit from having a broad set of data and measures that allow analysts to tap a wide range of theoretical constructs when modeling retention behavior. One of the most potent tools is a database that tracks customers' interactions with the firm.

If we believe that every interaction between the firm and the customer (or prospect) affects the customer's attitude and satisfaction with the firm, then this suggests the need for databases that track *all* customer (or prospect) interactions. Although every customer or prospect interaction may not generate revenue, each one can be linked to an expected or potential monetary value in the future.

Companies tend to collect very little customer interaction data. Consider a hypothetical frequent flyer who spends an average of $100,000 per year with an airline and has had several negative experiences. Several of the customer's flights were significantly delayed or canceled. The customer then had poor service from a flight attendant and responded to the airline with a negative letter. In the end, the customer found an alternative airline for most flights.

Should the airline have been able to detect such problems and forestall the defection? Clearly, the answer is yes, although it requires sophisticated database management to do so. For example, this airline could assign a customer retention specialist to be responsible for regularly obtaining from the operations department all information on canceled or delayed flights. This person then could match the information to individual customers by linking the frequent-flyer database to the operations database. Next, the retention specialist could append information from the customer complaint database. Once all three databases have been linked, the specialist could analyze the data to identify flyers whose travel patterns have changed or who are at risk for defection. This system also would make it possible for the specialist to recognize sources of customer dissatisfaction. After identifying them, the firm could develop communications, pricing, and promotional strategies to overcome the problems.

In contrast to the previous example, Toyota, the maker of Lexus, is an example of a firm that recognizes the importance of customer interaction data. Under the umbrella of the Lexus franchise, Toyota has pioneered an approach designed to make its dealer interactions more positive. For instance, Lexus monitors all service activity between the dealer and the customer. Lexus also has a policy under which a dealer's margins are dependent on the quality of its customer interactions. (Some European and U.S. automobile manufacturers have imitated this concept.) The result has been above average retention rates for Lexus. (Lexus has retention rates of about 75 percent, versus 50 percent in the U.S. automobile industry as a whole.)

Interaction databases should include the source of the interaction, the cause of the interaction, and the outcome of the interaction. Gathering this information is not simple, because many of the interaction data come from different functional areas within the firm, as we saw in the airline example. Furthermore, customers, not the firm, initiate many critical customer–firm interactions, lessening the firm's control over the information-gathering process.

The value of interaction data depends on their integration into a total customer-interaction database or data warehouse. Decisions made using an interaction database are decisions based on a more holistic view of the customer–firm relationship. Table 4-2 lists customer interactions that companies should track, along with the functional areas responsible for gathering the data.

## Measuring and Accounting for Retention

As defined in chapter 2, customer equity is the sum of acquisition equity, retention equity, and add-on selling equity. The net profits generated during the retention phase of the customer–firm relationship are what we call a firm's retention equity. Some firms use the term *lifetime value of a customer* to describe these retention profits, but this term may or may not include acquisition profit or loss. To avoid confusion and to distinguish between acquisition profitability (or loss) and retention profitability (or loss), we use the term *retention equity*.

**Table 4-2**
Example of Customer Interaction Data

| Customer Interaction | Data Tracked | Functional Area Responsible |
|---|---|---|
| Customer complaint | Complaint Resolution | Customer service |
| Sales (end user) | Sales | Accounting/Channel member |
| Market communication | Advertising sent Promotions sent Sales force calls | Marketing/Sales |
| Shipments, deliveries, operations | Fulfillment time Delays | Logistics |
| Product | Satisfaction Performance | Quality control |
| Invoicing | Billing | Accounting |
| Channel member (firm) | Sales Profits | Accounting |

There are two methods for calculating retention equity, which differ in how they determine the number of customers remaining at any given time. The first, more straightforward, method is based on traditional survival models; the second uses a recency, frequency, monetary value (RFM) model and involves more complicated computations.

### USING A SURVIVAL MODEL TO COMPUTE RETENTION EQUITY

A survival model calculates the probability distribution associated with how long a customer survives as a customer, and gives the probability that a customer will survive to a specific point in time. This probability, when combined with relevant revenue and cost data, makes it possible to compute the customer's retention value.

A simple survival model assumes that once a customer "dies"—stops buying—he or she will not purchase in the future. This may not always be a good assumption, and the analysis can be modified to account for reactivated customers.

Fundamentally, survival analysis calculates the probability that members of a group of customers, or cohort, will still be customers at a future point in time. It does so by starting with an estimate of the maximum retention rate the firm would attain if it spent an infinite amount on customer retention, and adjusting it to reflect the influence of the passage of time (and maturation of customer life cycles) on retention. A decision calculus procedure is used to arrive at these adjustments. Because the decision calculus approach relies on managerial input, the model's quality is only as good as the manager's judgment.

## USING AN RFM MODEL TO COMPUTE RETENTION EQUITY

The alternative to using a survival model to determine retention equity is to use an RFM model. An RFM model tracks customers through their purchase histories and groups customers into cells with similar purchase sizes, frequencies, and timing. It then predicts future customer behavior by cell. This type of modeling requires the use of decision trees, which are simple to understand but laborious to compute. Once analysts predict future purchase levels, they can compare them with costs to calculate retention equity.

No matter which method a firm uses, computing retention equity is a challenging task and may require sophisticated statistical assistance to ensure that the computations are as accurate as possible. Nonetheless, many different types of firms can, and do, undertake this task. These firms recognize that the resulting understanding of customer equity more than compensates for the effort.

## RETENTION MEASURES

Table 4-3 shows important summary statistics for retention:

- Number of current customers

- Number defected

- Percentage defected

- Duration-adjusted defection rate

- Duration-adjusted retention rate (1 minus the duration-adjusted defection rate)

Typical defection and retention rates are average rates, influenced equally by the retention rate of newer customers and the retention rate of customers who have had longer relationships with the firm. Of course, retention rates vary among the different stages of the cus-

**Table 4-3**

Customer Retention Accounting: Summary

| Year | Number of Current Customers | Number of Customers Defected | Percentage of Customers Defected | Duration-Adjusted Defection Rate (%) | Duration-Adjusted Retention Rate (%) |
|------|------|------|------|------|------|
| 1999 | 16,056 | 4,750 | 29.58 | 29.00 | 71.0 |
| 1998 | 15,341 | 4,100 | 26.73 | 34.00 | 66.0 |
| 1997 | 14,443 | 3,938 | 27.27 | 22.00 | 78.0 |
| 1996 | 14,103 | 3,413 | 24.20 | 19.00 | 81.0 |
| 1995 | 13,375 | 2,955 | 22.09 | 21.00 | 79.0 |
| 1994 | 12,449 | 3,133 | 25.17 | 23.00 | 77.0 |
| 1993 | 11,791 | 2,754 | 23.36 | 25.00 | 75.0 |
| 1992 | 11,104 | 2,488 | 22.41 | 21.00 | 79.0 |
| 1991 | 10,681 | 2,361 | 22.10 | 22.00 | 78.0 |
| 1990 | 9,983 | 2,115 | 21.19 | 24.00 | 76.0 |

tomer–firm relationship. Therefore, a firm's retention rate at any point in time can be strongly influenced by its acquisition strategy and by the distribution of its customers across the customer life cycle. For example, if a firm increases its focus on acquisition, its defection rate will rise because new customers generally have much higher defection rates than long-term customers do.

Duration-adjusted rates correct for such distortions. The duration adjustment is computed by standardizing the customer base and then normalizing the distribution of customer durations. In much of the popular business literature on retention, authors, consultants, and firms alike fail to make the proper adjustments to retention rates. However, some managers intuitively realize the impact that new customer acquisitions can have on retention rates. Management that is evaluated and compensated based on retention and defection rates has a tendency to avoid increasing acquisition rates, because it recognizes that retention rates likely will decline. The failure to acquire customers with a positive NPV ultimately reduces customer equity.

Companies should also measure the ratio of lost customers to new customers. This important metric indicates whether or not a firm is filling its pipeline with new customers as rapidly as it is losing them.

## *Data Analysis Tools for Retention*

Before it implements retention programs, a firm needs to determine which customer assets are worth retaining. The two primary tools for this are decile analysis and RFM analysis.

### DECILE ANALYSIS

The most common and most simple procedure for retention targeting is decile analysis. This method determines the relative profitability and sales of different customer segments. Firms that do not conduct decile analysis often are surprised to learn that a small percentage of customers represents a large percentage of the firm's profits and sales. Decile analysis also shows which individual customers are most valuable.

Deciles are 10 percent groupings computed by ranking each customer according to his or her purchases, or according to any other variable of interest, such as profitability, and grouping the customers into 10 percent segments. There is nothing magical about groups of 10 percent. Some firms prefer 5 percent groupings. Others prefer 1 percent groupings.

Typically, the top three deciles of customers represent anywhere from 60 percent to 80 percent of a firm's sales and profits. In retailing, for example—category by category and retailer by retailer—it appears that 30 percent of customers represent 70 percent of sales and profits.

The advantage of decile analysis is that it is extremely easy to construct and to execute. It is, however, very limited in scope. It does not capture most of the information available from the customer database, discriminate between new and old customers, or determine which customers have the most potential to increase their purchases. In short, it does not make the most use out of available information. Nonetheless, decile analysis can be a real eye-opener for a firm that has never conducted it.

### RFM ANALYSIS

In addition to its value in calculating retention equity, RFM analysis is an excellent predictor of future customer purchases. RFM analysis works well for almost any industry, and is very popular among direct marketing companies.

RFM analysis can be difficult to learn at first, even though it builds on a relatively simple concept. We begin by explaining how to use RFM analysis to describe the current state of a customer base, and then explain how to expand the analysis to include predictions about customer behavior.

*Computing Current Customer Status.* The purpose of an RFM matrix is to display how customers are distributed by purchase recency, frequency, and value. To create an RFM matrix:

1. Set cell definitions. RFM matrices commonly have recency as one axis of the matrix and frequency–monetary value as the other.

2. Determine the breaks for recency and frequency–monetary value. These breaks are very important to the quality of the RFM analysis. A simple histogram, which shows the distribution of each cell, often helps to identify a reasonable set of breaks. Analysts also should take purchase cycles into consideration. Using a product's purchase cycle as the average value for the first cell in recency and then setting the other breaks from there often works well. For the frequency variable, there should be a separate cell for one-time buyers. For the monetary value variable, breaks should increase as frequency increases.

3. Place every customer into one—and only one—cell, based on the customer's historical buying behavior. From this information, the analyst can compute the percentage of customers in each cell and determine the purchasing pattern.

*Computing Purchasing Probabilities.* An RFM matrix can be used to predict future purchase rates. To do so:

1. Define and populate the cells, as explained in the previous subsection.

2. For a given time period, track each customer in a cell to see if he or she purchases. (A customer who purchases more than once during the purchasing period is recorded as purchasing only once.)

3. For each cell, compute the fraction of customers in the cell who purchased during the observed period. This fraction is an estimate of the cell's purchasing probability for the next time period. If a product is seasonal, adjust the base and purchasing periods accordingly.

*Advantages and Disadvantages of RFM Analysis.* The RFM framework is an effective method for summarizing and interpreting complex purchase data. In general, RFM analysis is a simple but useful way to characterize customers (which makes it useful for determining customer life cycles). It is highly predictive, and it focuses on actual buyer behavior, not one demographic type or industry code.

RFM does have several drawbacks. First, it cannot easily incorporate product affinity or customer demographics. Second, it may be less useful for infrequently purchased goods, because in those cases the ability to predict diminishes significantly. Third, RFM analysis ignores the *reference value* of a customer. Specifically, this refers to the positive or negative impact that a customer can have on other customers. MCI's "Friends and Family" promotion is an example of this type of value.

## Targeting Defectors

Relatively few simple methods exist for identifying defectors, which makes this area the least developed set of techniques for managing customer equity. This section briefly describes how to use the recency–sales rate (RS) matrix to target defectors and then discusses some more advanced techniques.

### THE RS MATRIX

Using an RS matrix (a tool similar to the RFM matrix) is the easiest way to target defectors. The basic idea is that a customer's sales rate and recency tell us something about whether the customer will repurchase.

Customers included in an RS matrix have to have made enough purchases to indicate a purchasing pattern. Generally speaking, analysts should not classify as defectors newer customers who have made only one or even two purchases. A defector is someone who was a regular customer and is no longer.

To build an RS matrix, include customers who have made at least three purchases and compute three statistics for each of these customers:

1. Recency (the time elapsed since the customer's last purchase)

2. The sales rate of the customer per period (total time since a customer's first purchase divided by the number of times purchased)

3. The number of periods that will elapse until the customer is likely to repurchase (the second statistic divided into 1)

If the recency of the customer is greater than the third statistic (that is, if the customer has not bought within this predicted amount of time), then the customer likely is a defector.

An RS matrix is a relatively simple system for identifying defectors and has many of the same advantages that an RFM matrix does. It is easy to interpret and to construct. If a product or service has a moderately frequent and regular purchase cycle, the RS matrix can quickly identify defectors.

Of course, the RS matrix has some limitations. It is less useful if the firm has not been able to observe a full purchase cycle for customers. Also, it is dependent on the firm's ability to determine the recency variable's appropriate intervals accurately. In addition, the RS method does not incorporate other variables that can predict the likelihood of defection.

## STATISTICAL MODELS

Statistical modeling is a more sophisticated way to predict defectors. One model type, a logit model, is commonly used to identify variables affecting the probability of an event. In our case, the event is defection.

Logit models depend on specific independent variables. For example, when measuring defectors, possible independent variables include the ratio of the purchase cycle to the time since last purchase, the number of purchases, how much the customer has spent in total, changes in price, and changes in promotional activity. Other variables can include the number of different products or services purchased by the customer, specific customer service problems, change of address, or other indicators that could cause the customer to change buying behavior.

The benefit of a logit model is that it can include explanatory variables, which makes it significantly more powerful than an RS matrix. A logit model allows a firm to assess the impact of other variables besides recency and sales rate on a customer's likelihood of defection. If these variables have significant explanatory power, the firm should be able to improve the accuracy with which it predicts defectors in its customer base, and should be able to take action to prevent economic losses caused by actions such as targeting nondefectors with price promotions. In short, a logit model can be a very powerful analytical tool.

On the downside, a logit model demands a great deal of skill from its users. The average analyst cannot set up or run the technique—specialists are required. This can be a big drawback for firms that are considering the use of logit models.

## Summary

As should be obvious by now, customer retention is a crucial element of customer equity management. However, managers need to remember that the goal is to maximize customer equity, not retention. They also need to remember that retention generally comes at a cost, which should be factored into any analysis of what retention rate to target, as well as into the choice of specific retention tactics.

# 5

---

# Enhancing Customer Equity
# through Add-on Selling

I BM, DURING ITS halcyon years, developed a compensation system for
its sales force that rewarded "installed-base" selling, that is, selling to
existing customers. If a customer owned an 1108 or another IBM mainframe computer model, the sales force was expected to sell this customer
not only additional computer hardware, but also peripheral equipment,
including disk and tape drives, punch cards, and other relevant products
and services. IBM's strategy was not just to capture new customers and
retain them, but also to increase revenue per customer. We call the latter strategy enhancing customer equity through add-on selling.

## Defining Add-on Selling

Most managers confuse add-on selling with cross-selling. However,
add-on selling is broader than cross-selling: It includes cross-selling,
but is not limited to it. Cross-selling depends on specific interactions or
relationships between products. Add-on selling does not. Selling print-
ers with personal computers is an example of cross-selling. Add-on selling is closer to the concept of installed-base selling, which IBM used so
effectively in the 1950s and 1960s when it required its sales force to sell
additional products to its customer base. Add-on selling is the activity
associated with selling any additional products and services to current
customers.

For example, if a telecommunications company sells voice mail to its customers, that qualifies as both add-on selling and cross-selling. In contrast, when AT&T created the Universal Card, that was not cross-selling, because there was no relationship between the card and AT&T's other products at the time. But it was add-on selling, because the card was targeted to AT&T's current user base.

## The Role of Add-on Selling in Customer Equity Management

The most obvious role of add-on selling is its ability to directly increase customer equity through higher profits per customer. But the impact of add-on selling is much broader. How? One of the key rules of acquisition is that the greater the back-end profits (profits per retained customer over time), the more a firm can invest in customer acquisition. This means that successful add-on selling can allow a firm to increase investment in customer acquisition because the cost of selling additional products to current customers is generally lower and thus profits are higher.

Add-on selling has long been the neglected stepchild of marketing. Companies practice it, but they rarely have understood how to integrate it into a comprehensive marketing strategy. Many "old economy" companies develop add-on selling programs only after the customer base begins to mature. "New economy," Web-based companies seem to have a better understanding of add-on selling's potential. They tend to market additional products and services to newly acquired customers as quickly as possible. Amazon.com and Yahoo! are prime examples.

Firms in other industries, such as finance, appear to be learning. An ex-CEO of Citibank developed a strategy in which the credit card division would acquire customers, and then other divisions would cross-sell to them. First Horizon (also called First Tennessee Bank) uses mortgages as its acquisition product line and then cross-sells other financial services to its customers.

## The Add-on Selling Process

To successfully add-on sell, a firm needs to identify the best products or services to offer its customer base. Many firms fail to recognize their add-on selling opportunities because they do not adequately research their customer bases and customer affinities. The case study of The Sports Expert Online in the following section is an example of a firm that engaged in extensive research about their customer database. This research led to a comprehensive add-on selling strategy that matched the appropriate product to the right consumers.

Figure 5-1 describes the add-on selling process. First, a firm needs to identify the products or services it can offer to its customer base. Next, it targets its customers with products, offers, and prices, which results in a purchase or no-purchase response. To this basic structure, we add two more elements, based on key issues in customer equity management: customer satisfaction; and the lock-in effect of increasing the number of products that a customer purchases from a firm, which in other words means increasing the number of the customer's relationships with the firm. Both of these added elements affect retention, although the extent to which they do so is the subject of some debate.

## Case Study: The Sports Expert Online, Inc.

In 1999, Central Publishing Incorporated, a U.S. publisher of a national sports magazine, *Sports Expert* (name disguised), had a subscriber base of 1.2 million. *Sports Expert* had an unprecedented reputation for accurate and up-to-date content, award-winning editorials, and prestigious association with well-known athletes and sports analysts. In addition to the *Sports Expert* magazine, the company also launched a Sports Expert Web site in the first quarter of 1999. During the first three years of publication, management's focus had been to build top-line revenue and establish a solid subscriber base. Recognizing that the Sports Expert business had developed a substantial loyal base of subscribers, the parent company began to focus on the profits generated by this business unit.

On the road to building a profit margin of 35 percent (current margins totaled 20 percent), management quickly changed from a strategy that maximized the number of its subscribers and revenues to a strategy that aimed to maximize company profits. Through its analysis of its core product and service offering, the company's business-to-business Strategic Alliance Partnership Program (SAPP) offering came under scrutiny.

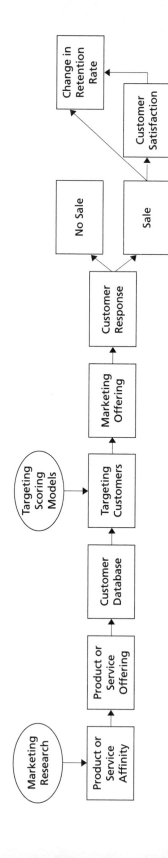

**Figure 5-1** The Add-on Selling Process

## Strategic Alliance Partnership Program

Through the SAPP offering, Sports Expert provided its partners with rich sports content for their Web sites. Typical SAPP partners included sports retailers, sports venues, professional and amateur sports franchises, and online sports communities. In return for content that enhanced their respective Web sites, the business partner would provide Sports Expert with an additional branding opportunity (the content header stated "Sports information brought to you by the Sports Expert"), a monthly fee, and a link to the publication's Web site. Thus, for Sports Expert, SAPP served as a distribution channel for gaining new subscribers, additional brand exposure, and a steady revenue stream from monthly fees.

Sports Expert offered three different options under the SAP Program—Level I, Level II, and Level III—that varied in complexity, richness of the content, and price. Level I, the company's core SAPP product, simply enabled the business customer to post a limited number of top sports news stories on their site. In addition to these top sports stories, a Level II SAPP provided the business clients with more customized content targeted to the business client's primary customer base. For example, the Sports Expert would deliver sports stories related to female athletes for its partnership with a retailer that sold only women's athletic apparel. In addition to the content offered under the Level I and Level II programs, a Level III SAPP offered even greater customization to the business client by providing the business client's website visitors with local sports content. As a result, when a visitor logged in to a site from San Francisco, he or she would see sports content relating to the San Francisco Giants, the San Francisco 49ers, and local college sports.

Although the Sports Expert received a monthly fee from its partners in the SAPP, the significant majority of revenues were attributed to the new number of subscribers that were generated when a consumer linked through a partner to the Sports Expert Web site and signed up for a subscription to the magazine. In addition, the monthly fee did not cover all of the costs associated with creating and building the content that was provided to business partners. As a result, the revenues that were gained through new subscriptions resulting from the SAP Program were integral to the profitability of each partnership contract. Although management was aware that the entire SAP Program produced profits for Sports Expert, they were not confident about the profitability of the individual business alliances.

To assess the profitability of the program, the account management team hired a sales consulting firm, L&E Incorporated. L&E analyzed the SAP Program in totality, each specific level offering, and each business-to-business contract. The results of the analysis indicated that the margin amounts per level varied (table 5-1). The consultants also identified that less than 50 percent of the partnerships were actually profitable (table 5-2).

### Analysis by Contract and by Level

Through discussions with many of Sports Expert's account managers, L&E discovered that the sales team was often unaware of the profit (or lack of profit) that each of their SAPP contract deals generated. Typically, the client chose the SAPP level it preferred without the guidance of the account manager. At this point in time, account managers were uncertain of the level of subscribers needed to better ensure that each SAPP contract was profitable. However, the break-even analysis (table 5-3) performed by the consultants clearly identified the number of subscribers needed per SAPP level to guarantee that Sports Expert would generate profits from the deal.

Consequently, the account managers could now target an appropriate SAPP level for new clients based on an evaluation of the client's ability to generate potential subscribers. As a result of the increasing margins in the more complex product offering, the analysis also illustrated the value of "up-selling" the clients from the core product (Level I).

### Add-on Selling Opportunity . . . or Not?

Encouraging a client over time to purchase more products and services or to purchase a more expensive version of a product is a typical add-on selling strategy by many firms; however, Sports Expert's more complex revenue model would require a unique strategy that would guarantee profitability at all levels and for all client contracts. The break-even numbers clearly indicated what subscriber number would be required for a business client to qualify for the more enhanced SAPP products. Clients that had been able to consistently provide the appropriate number of subscribers per level were identified as prime sales candidates for the more complex SAPP levels (table 5-4). In contrast, clients that had been unable to provide an adequate number of subscribers per month would not be encouraged to purchase a higher-level program even if the client was willing to pay the larger monthly fee.

**Table 5-1**
Margins for SAPP Levels

| SAPP Product | Total Costs per Month ($) | Monthly Fee Revenue | No. of Subscribers | Subscriber Revenue per Subscriber | Total Subscriber Revenues | Total Revenue | Profit | Gross Margin (%) |
|---|---|---|---|---|---|---|---|---|
| Level I: 5 clients | 5,000 | 1,000 | 375 | 19.95 | 7,481 | 8,481 | 3,481 | 41 |
| Level II: 10 clients | 27,500 | 3,000 | 2,000 | 19.95 | 39,900 | 42,900 | 15,400 | 36 |
| Level III: 8 clients | 40,000 | 4,000 | 3,200 | 19.95 | 63,840 | 67,840 | 27,840 | 41 |
| Total | 72,500 | 8,000 | 5,575 | | 111,221 | 119,221 | 46,721 | 39 |

**Table 5-2**
Profit/Loss per Partnership

| | Subscribers | Break-even No. of Subscribers | Profit/Loss ($) |
|---|---|---|---|
| LEVEL I CLIENTS | | | |
| Athlete Express | 30 | 40 | (199.50) |
| Healthtrac | 104 | 40 | 1,276.80 |
| Playtron | 99 | 40 | 1,177.05 |
| SS Footwear | 26 | 40 | (279.30) |
| Squad Inc. | 112 | 40 | 1,436.40 |
| LEVEL II CLIENTS | | | |
| Sports Town | 189 | 122 | 1,336.65 |
| Competitor Inc. | 76 | 122 | (917.70) |
| Outdoor Sports Inc. | 67 | 122 | (1,097.25) |
| Excellerate | 212 | 122 | 1,795.50 |
| Team Baseball | 112 | 122 | (199.50) |
| Runners Unlimited | 193 | 122 | 1,416.45 |
| Traintrek | 55 | 122 | (1,336.65) |
| Top Notch | 135 | 122 | 259.35 |
| Central Zone | 95 | 122 | (538.65) |
| Superbuy Outlets | 87 | 122 | (698.25) |
| LEVEL III CLIENTS | | | |
| Soccer Elite | 250 | 225 | 498.75 |
| Sports & Health | 178 | 225 | (937.65) |
| Batter's Box | 150 | 225 | (1,496.25) |
| SuperiorSports | 280 | 225 | 1,097.25 |
| Power One | 245 | 225 | 399.00 |
| The Front Runner | 167 | 225 | (1,157.10) |
| SuperiorExpress | 309 | 225 | 1,675.80 |
| Blue Banner | 220 | 225 | (99.75) |

## *A Consistent SAPP Sales Strategy*

L&E Incorporated designed a sales strategy for the SAP Program that would identify what criteria were needed for a new SAPP client, identify the most beneficial opportunities for add-on selling, and identify unprofitable contracts and a process to improve profitability. The completed strategy is illustrated in table 5-5.

**Table 5-3**
Break-even Analysis

| Level | Break-even No. of Subscribers | |
|---|---|---|
| Level I | 40 | |
| Level II | 122 | |
| Level III | | 225 |

**Table 5-4**
Add-on Selling Opportunities

| | Current Subscribers | Break-even No. of Subscribers for New Level |
|---|---|---|
| LEVEL I ACCOUNTS TO LEVEL II | | |
| Squad Inc. | 112 | 122 |
| Healthtrac | 104 | 122 |
| LEVEL II ACCOUNTS TO LEVEL III | | |
| Excellerate | 212 | 225 |
| Sports Town | 189 | 225 |
| Runners Corp. | 193 | 225 |

In consideration of L&E's recommendation, the Sports Expert management team realized that a targeted sales strategy that cultivated profitability of the SAP Program at each level would ensure profit maximization for the SAP Program as a whole. Next steps included assessment of the implementation of the targeted sales strategy for the SAP Program and consideration of how a more targeted sales strategy might prove beneficial for other parts of Central Publishing Inc.'s business ventures.

## Determining the Value of Add-on Selling

The value of a firm's add-on selling efforts depends on many factors: the number of add-on offers a firm can economically provide per period, the response rate to these product offers, sales quantity per offer, how much it costs the company to make the offers, the size of the customer universe to which the firm can add-on sell, and the margins on the offered products.

**Table 5-5**
Sales Strategy for the SAP Program

| Criteria | Analysis Evaluated | Sales Strategy if Client Is Profitable | Sales Strategy if Client Is Unprofitable |
|---|---|---|---|
| Targeting potential SAPP clients | Evaluate the prospect's probability of generating the break-even number of subscribers. | If probability of generating 40 subscribers is over 90%, prospect is targeted for an SAPP sale. | If probability of generating 40 subscribers is less than 90%, prospect is not targeted for an SAPP sale but instead is periodically evaluated to see if probability changes. |
| 0–6 months: The initial sale— Level I | During the six months, account manager evaluates if a break-even number of 40 subscribers is achieved. | Add-on sell client to a more profitable level. | Generate creative solutions to assist the client with generating higher subscriber numbers *or* do not renew contract. |
| Level II and III clients | Clients are evaluated every six months to assess the trends in subscriber numbers. | Add-on sell Level II clients to Level III clients. If Level III: Assist client with strategies that will maintain current subscriber base. | Generate creative solutions to assist the client with generating higher subscriber numbers *or* drop client to Level I or Level II. |

## Number of Offers

One of the most important elements of add-on selling is the number of feasible offers a firm can make to its customers. In general, this number depends on the types of products or services that the firm offers; the firm's ability to create or acquire products (R&D); the firm's ability to create and manage a customer database; and the economic payout associated with marketing additional products and services to customers, which in turn is related to the response rate. Figure 5-2 shows these relationships visually.

Unlike some elements of add-on selling, the number of offers made to customers reflects strategic as well as tactical thinking. The make-or-buy decision plays an important role. Firms have the option of buying from outside companies the products or services they will add-on sell to their customers. We will discuss the issues involved in the make-or-buy decision in a later section of this chapter.

## Response Rate

The response rate affects the cost of making offers to customers. It also has a critical impact on customer equity: The higher the response rate to add-on selling, the lower the cost per customer of add-on selling and, as a result, the more offers a firm can make and the greater the add-on selling profits it will realize.

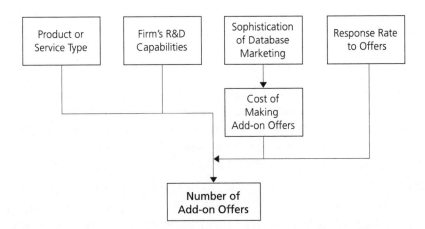

**Figure 5-2**  Factors Affecting the Number of Add-on Offers Made

Five primary factors determine the response rate, as shown in figure 5-3:

1. *The value of the product or service:* The higher the perceived value, the higher the response rate.

2. *How the product fits in with the firm's other products:* The greater the fit with the firm's other products, the more likely it is that the consumer will attribute expertise to the firm in that product area. The result is a higher response rate.

3. *The affinity the customer has with the firm:* The higher the affinity, the higher the response rate.

4. *The total expenditure for the offered product:* Generally, the higher the total expenditure, the lower the response rate.

5. *Specific marketing communications aimed at the customer:* The better targeted and positioned the messages, the higher the response rate.

Customer service and general image advertising also affect the response rate.

### Sales Quantity per Offer

Sometimes the total unit sales volume from an offer is low even though the offer response rate is high. This happens when the sales quantity purchased per offer is low. The type of product offered and its dollar value affect sales quantity. These are both, in turn, tactical variables that the firm determines. Keep in mind that the higher the expenditure per transaction, the lower the response rate.

### Marketing Cost per Offer

The determinants of cost per offer are the use of database marketing techniques (how efficiently the company reaches the customer), the type of product or service offered, and the type of customers being targeted. Figure 5-4 depicts these relationships.

Database marketing and other techniques that improve efficiency play very important roles in reaching customers. If a firm does not have a customer database, then the only way to add-on sell is to use mass marketing techniques, which in many instances are highly inefficient. Consumer-product firms such as Procter & Gamble are at a major

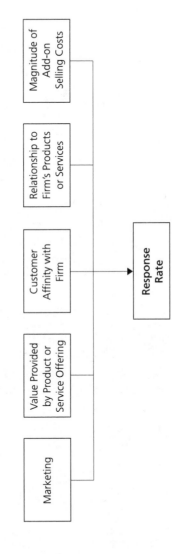

**Figure 5-3** Determinants of Add-on Selling Response Rates

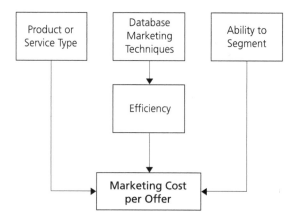

**Figure 5-4** Determinants of Add-on Selling Cost per Offer

disadvantage when it comes to add-on selling. They use very efficient channels of distribution, but they cannot obtain customer databases cost-effectively. This limits their ability to target customers for add-on selling. In contrast, retailers have frequent-shopper databases and are able to develop sophisticated add-on selling programs.

### Margin

The type of product or service offered and the cost of manufacturing or providing it determine the margin percentage. Some firms have learned that it can be highly advantageous to have lower margins but more products to offer. They accomplish this by acquiring their products or services from third parties. Sears, for example, leases services and whole departments to outside contractors. Dell manufactures almost none of its products. Making the product or service increases margins, but decreases the total number of products or services the company can provide to customers.

## Customer Affinity

Customer affinity is a combination of the relationship a customer has with a firm and the expertise that the customer believes the firm possesses (figure 5-5). The concept of customer affinity flows from the premise that a firm can apply its customer relationships and customers' perceptions of its expertise to related products. Branding can

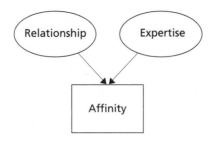

**Figure 5-5** Determinants of Affinity

contribute to affinity in that it helps to build customer–firm relationships and to create perceptions of quality and expertise among consumers.

In terms of specific cause and effect, affinity affects add-on sales through two interconnected variables: the number of offers a firm can make to customers, and the response rate. As customer affinity increases, customers become more confident in a firm's ability to meet their needs for quality and service, and more willing to try the firm's new products. Therefore a firm with greater customer affinity can expect higher response rates and can increase the number and type of its offers.

The breadth of products or services a firm can market to its customer base is also guided by the firm's customer affinity. A clothing cataloger, for instance, would have great difficulty selling Jaguars, no matter how strong its customer relationships. No one would believe that the catalog company has the requisite expertise in car sales or maintenance. Federal Express offers a less extreme example. When the company decided to provide rapid and guaranteed delivery of time-sensitive parts, its prior relationship with its customers and its expertise in providing overnight package delivery translated into customer willingness to purchase the new service. Customers had confidence in Federal Express's ability to deliver goods—packages or parts—quickly. But when Federal Express created ZapMail, an e-mail service, customers did not show the same willingness to purchase. The company's strong relationship with its customers could not overcome its perceived lack of expertise in electronic mail services.

### Recognizable Expertise

Expertise is similar to core competencies, but broader. In a customer affinity context, expertise does not matter unless customers recognize it. Furthermore, expertise serves to differentiate firms from each other. Consumers think of UPS, for example, as a package delivery company, whereas they think of Federal Express as an overnight express delivery company.

Expertise also resembles positioning in classical marketing, but it is tangible and unique, and customers have to consider it executable by the firm. For many years, United Airlines advertised friendly service, but did customers believe it could deliver on that promise?

A company's expertise should have salience across product lines. Microsoft entered the browser market with expertise in operating software and office software. This turned out to be a controversial move, but in terms of extending expertise to other products, it worked quite well. Customers perceived that Microsoft's expertise applied to the development of an Internet browser. This perception of expertise was bolstered by Microsoft's strong relationship with its customers: Many had already purchased more than one type of Microsoft product and were willing to try another.

### *Managing and Delivering on Customer Expectations*

To understand customer affinity well, a firm needs to recognize the importance of customer expectations. If a company meets expectations, it can build strong relationships with its customers. The firm does not have to provide maximum customer service or the highest-quality product; it does have to deliver on the specific expectations it has nurtured among its customers.

Southwest Airlines is a good example of a company that manages expectations effectively and provides service consistent with those expectations. It does not provide the highest service level: It offers neither a first-class section nor preassigned seating. But Southwest does not tell its customers it will offer those services. It meets expectations through low fares, an excellent on-time record, and good baggage handling. Its customers generally give it the highest service-quality ratings, and it is one of the most profitable airlines in the United States.

The affinity Southwest has created with a segment of customers should allow it to add products or services. It has demonstrated expertise in creating low-cost, efficient operational systems that provide a prespecified level of service to consumers. If Southwest can transfer the relationship it has with its customers and its expertise to other products or services, then it can add-on sell. To date, however, Southwest has decided to grow through the expansion of its current service offering into new markets, not through add-on services.

## Managing Customer Affinity

There are five steps to managing customer affinity:

1. *Internal assessment:* Identify the firm's core competencies.

2. *Internal process:* Translate these core competencies into an expertise.

3. *Marketing research:* Evaluate whether this expertise is salient to customers and apply it across product lines.

4. *Marketing research:* Evaluate the quality of the firm's relationship with its customers to determine if it is positive and strong.

5. *Product development:* Identify products and services that can be sold as add-on products.

We will use Time Life Books as an example. Time Life (now Time Warner) knew how to gather information and publish it. It had expertise in magazine journalism and an archive of historical information. Customers had relationships with *Time* and *Life* magazines that had developed over years of reading them as sources for current affairs information, great photography, and vignettes. Time translated these strengths into customer affinity and created a book series that tapped into it. The series covered a range of topics, many of which involved history or practical living. Some might simply call this an example of product-line extension, and to a certain extent they would be right. It is product-line extension guided by analysis of particular criteria: the firm's recognized expertise in journalism, photography, and information gathering, and its strong customer–firm relationship.

By some accounts, Oprah Winfrey can be thought of as the connoisseur of add-on selling. Her success across multiple product and service categories demonstrates that she clearly understands the value of add-on selling and how to leverage customer affinity. The following case study details her most recent venture into the magazine business.

## Case Study: Oprah and Add-on Selling

The most significant player in the magazine business in the United States is someone who has never published a magazine before. This "company" epitomizes the way to take advantage of high customer equity to make add-on sales, which further increase customer equity. The new magazine is called *O*, and the "company" that produces this magazine is Oprah Winfrey, most famous as a daytime TV talk show host. The audience for this magazine is predominantly women, most of whom are fans of Oprah's television show.

As of October 2000, *O* was the best-selling magazine in the United States:

- Newsstand sales averaged 5.5 million copies, according to Hearst—more than the average newsstand sales of *Time* and more than the newsstand sales of *Vogue*, *Self*, and *Martha Stewart Living* combined.

- After just four issues, *O* already had more than a million subscribers, according to Hearst, which is appreciably more than long-established magazines such as *Vogue* (681,000, according to the Audit Bureau) and *Self* (786,000) and even more than the relatively recent upstart *In Style* (646,000) (see figure 5-6).

- Seventy-five percent of all *O* copies placed on newsstands around the country are sold, compared with an average of 50 percent for other successful magazines, such as *Time*, *Newsweek*, and *People*.

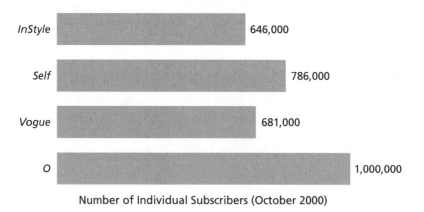

**Figure 5-6**   Subscription Rates of Major Magazines

- 210,000 subscriptions had come in through Oprah.com, making the Web site probably the most successful example to date of a closely watched source of magazine subscriptions.

The *O* magazine is Winfrey's latest and most successful add-on venture. Previous to the launch of her magazine, Winfrey has capitalized on her popularity to sell and promote books, movies, television specials, a cable channel, and a Web site. In all of these ventures, she skillfully targets her existing customers—her viewers—to promote her add-on selling offerings.

The success of Oprah's add-on selling ventures demonstrates that successful add-on selling efforts require a firm to understand the value of the products or services for its customers, create a strong customer affinity, manage and deliver on customer expectations, demonstrate that the product fits with the firm's other products, and use specific marketing communications aimed at the customer.

### The Value of Products and Services

*The Oprah Show* show is a departure from other daytime talk shows. Unlike other daytime shows, which feature sensational stories of Satanists, cross-dressers, racists, and exhibitionists, *The Oprah Show is* focused on improvement and empowerment of women, her target audience.

For viewers who enjoy *The Oprah Show*, each additional product Winfrey sells provides further sources of enjoyment. Many of the topics featured on the show are also featured in the magazine. For instance, when Winfrey airs a show featuring a beloved celebrity, she often features that celebrity in *O*. A reader can enjoy the additional details of a celebrity's likes and dislikes. Viewers also get a closer, more familiar glimpse into Winfrey. She often writes about her likes and dislikes, joys and fears (in the form of personal narratives) in much more detail than she reveals on the show. Since Oprah often plays a role in the television specials she produces, viewers get a chance to see her perform.

### Customer Affinity

Each week an estimated twenty-two million viewers tune into *The Oprah Show*. Since the show's national debut in September 1986, it has become the number one rated daytime television show in the history of television, winning thirty-two Emmy awards.

As evidenced by her television ratings, Winfrey has managed to secure a strong affinity with her viewers/customers. This affinity is due in part to her sharing the most intimate aspects of her life. Stories of her humble beginning as a poor African-American child in Mississippi, her survival of child abuse, her lifelong battle with her weight, and her relationship with her fiancé, Stedman Graham, are a few examples of her intimate disclosures. Her willingness to disclose these details enables her audience to identify and empathize with her every trial and build a personal bond. This intimate bond directly translates into her ability to add-on sell.

### Managing and Delivering on Customer Expectations

Customers are confident that each new product Winfrey endorses will be a high-quality product and one that has their needs in mind. When a reader picks up an edition of *O* or a viewer turns on *The Oprah Show*, he or she expects to see Oprah. Readers are well aware that she is very involved with the publication. Every edition of *O* has between ten and fifteen pictures of Oprah, from the cover to the final column. She authors editorials and columns for each edition. Readers sense the overall match in look and feel of the magazine and the show.

### How O Fits with the Firm's Other Products

Oprah Winfrey's portfolio of products—*O*, Oprah's Book Club, Oxygen Media, and Harpo Productions—reflects the core messages of her shows: improvement and empowerment.

The *O* magazine acts as an extension of *The Oprah Show*. Many of the common guests on the show have regular columns in the magazine. For instance, Dr. Phil McGraw, a clinical psychologist who frequently discusses relationship issues on the show, has a regular feature in the magazine, "Tell It Like It Is," in which he dispenses relationship advice Dear-Abby style. Gary Zukav, a new age philosopher and author who also appears regularly on the show, writes a monthly column for the magazine detailing his new observations. Suze Orman, a financial expert who appears at least bimonthly on the show, has a regular monthly feature on money management entitled "Financial Freedom" in the magazine. Oprah, as editor in chief of the magazine, writes a regular feature toward the end of the magazine, "What I Know for Sure"—the same feature seen on the show.

## Specific Marketing Communications Aimed at the Customer

*O* is not marketed one-to-one to the customer. Rather, Oprah Winfrey makes personal appeals to her customers on her show and her Web site. Although she rarely openly plugs her magazine or newest television special on the air, Winfrey encourages viewers/customers to connect with one another and discuss themes prevalent in the magazine or the special. By purchasing a book featured on Oprah's Book Club, watching any of the movie or television specials she has produced, or purchasing *O*, a customer immediately feels like part of a community.

Winfrey increases the value of her customer equity through community building. She makes investments in her customers. Winfrey uses her show to encourage her customers to relay their experiences with her and one another through her Web site. At Oprah.com, she welcomes her customers to discuss any of the issues apparent in any of her works. For instance, if a customer reads an article on volunteerism in the magazine, he or she may be inspired to go online and connect with other customers in the area who are also interested in volunteerism. The sense of community she fosters with her viewers on the show is translated to her other products.

## The Make-or-Buy Decision for Add-on Selling

Add-on selling has tended to be product driven. A firm's research and development team determines if there are other products that the firm can make and sell to its customers. But this model is changing rapidly as firms learn either to create strategic alliances or to serve as marketing conduits for other firms' products and services. Internet portals (such as Yahoo!) that serve as matchmakers but manufacture nothing are prime examples of this new trend. Similarly, America Online uses its immense customer base to market products for a fee plus a percentage of revenues.

The concept of serving as a matchmaker rather than a producer has become a prominent part of the so-called new economy. It also exemplifies an important lesson of customer equity management: Decision making must focus on the customer, not on a firm's legacy of production. This is a very hard lesson for traditional firms. The culture of product-centric companies changes slowly and reluctantly.

All that said, the decision to make or buy is not simple. Earlier we emphasized the opportunity that acquiring or marketing other products and services presents, but it is extremely difficult to outsource production to third parties. On a general level, the following premise should guide the make-or-buy decision: Customers are a firm's key asset, and selling products that deplete this asset violate the firm's basic economic goal, which is to increase customer equity.

On a more specific level, a firm should consider the following factors when deciding whether to make or buy products for add-on selling:

- *The level and uncertainty of demand for products or services:* Acquiring a product from third parties reduces the risk posed by possible low demand. The following rule works well: Outsource the add-on product or service if expected demand is low or the risk relative to expected demand is high.

- *The firm's expertise in manufacturing products or providing services:* Many firms have limited expertise in manufacturing products that are not core to their production systems or operations. Unfortunately, many firms are bound by their production expertise and want to exploit it. As a result, they miss significant opportunities to enhance customer equity.

- *The firm's ability to manage outsourcing:* Some firms recognize the need to outsource. They create procurement teams responsible for identifying products, evaluating them, and then monitoring their quality. If a firm is weak in this area, it likely will fail to provide customers with quality, cost-effective products and services and as a result will lower its customer equity.

- *The quality of outsourced products or services:* If the outsourced product or service falls below required standards, the firm will face serious backlash from its customers and a consequent loss of customer equity. Firms can solve this problem through sophisticated quality control system requirements similar to the requirements that many original equipment manufacturers (OEMs) have placed on their suppliers.

- *The risks of outsourcing:* Risks of outsourcing include supplier's bankruptcy; supplier's change of ownership, resulting in changes in costs or, more likely, changes in quality control; varying quality; rising costs if there are few suppliers in the market; and product liability. By assigning a team of managers from different functional areas (e.g., finance, legal, production, marketing) to oversee the outsourcing agreement, a firm can reduce the risks of outsourcing.

- *The cost structure for internal production or service provision versus the cost of acquiring products or services:* Assessing the costs of outsourcing requires a comprehensive understanding of incremental, semi-incremental, and fixed costs. Many firms look at their in-house production costs on a fully loaded basis, but their true costs are significantly lower. On the flip side, many do not take into account hidden administrative and management expenses when evaluating outside production costs. The flexibility of outside production also affects costs. If a firm contracts for production on a variable-cost basis and demand declines or is below expectations, then the producer accepts the risk. Also, because in many situations outside producers view the production as additional incremental volume, they might be more willing to offer low prices that cover incremental costs and provide some profit margin. These lower costs can be difficult for internal production teams to meet if they do not identify costs as incremental, semivariable, or fixed.

Deciding whether to outsource production of add-on products and services is a very important decision. It should not be made according to a firm's philosophy. It is a business decision. In today's business environment, more and more firms have become willing to outsource production. They recognize that it is better to sell a customer incremental products than to allow another firm to capture the revenue and profits.

## The Relationship among Add-on Selling, Retention Rates, and Customer Value

Firms and consultants tout that the more relationships a customer has with a company, the higher the retention rate and the higher the customer lifetime value. Consider this excerpt from an analyst's report on Yahoo!:

A variety of personalized offerings ranging from My Yahoo! to Yahoo! Calendar to Yahoo! Messenger are all designed to create stickiness and reduce churn. Management estimates that once a user taps into three or more services, churn is reduced significantly, enabling the company to expand its base and drive incremental revenues.[1]

This statement has very important strategic implications. Linking add-on selling to retention and customer lifetime value clearly affects financial analysis of the add-on selling investment. However, given that response rates to add-on offers differ across individuals, a fundamental challenge in developing a profitable add-on selling strategy is determining which customers to target for offers. This issue is of paramount importance for firms whose customer database can be characterized by some approximation of the 80-20 rule (20 percent of the customers contribute 80 percent of the profits).

Research by Thomas and Reinartz examines the effect of cross-buying (buying from multiple product categories) on relationship duration and customer lifetime value.[2] Specifically, the research examines how the impact of cross-buying differs for customers with varying levels of recency, frequency, and the monetary value of their last purchase. The preliminary analysis shows that cross-buying increases retention for all customers, but most for more recent, less frequent, and low monetary value customers. This result is important because firms generally target their add-on selling efforts to the more recent, more frequent, and higher monetary value customers. Counter to this behavior, the analysis implies that firms can affect their retention rates more by targeting customers who purchase less frequently and whose last purchase had a low monetary value.

In terms of customer lifetime value, the preliminary analysis indicates that the impact of add-on buying is generally greatest for the more recent and more frequent customers. The results with regard to the monetary value of the customer's last purchase were less conclusive. However, the general trend that is uncovered is that the impact of cross-buying on enhancing customer profitability is greatest for customers whose last purchases had lower monetary values. This result suggests that it is not always easier to increase the value of higher-value customers. Holding all other factors constant, in some instances firms have a higher probability of improving the lifetime value of a customer with lower monetary value than a customer whose last purchase had a high value.

The research also shows that the differential impact of cross-buying on retention and lifetime value has important implications for the firm's cross-selling strategy. Although cross-buying positively affects both the relationship duration (i.e., retention) and the customer's profitability (i.e., lifetime value), firms must determine their primary objective for add-on selling (i.e., enhancing relationship duration or improving customer profitability) and then target those customers who will best help them to attain that objective.

## Methods and Tools for Add-on Selling

### Databases for Add-on Selling

Customer databases and database marketing technology should improve both the efficiency and the effectiveness of add-on selling. They support more efficient targeting of prospective buyers (from the customer file) and greater effectiveness in developing the appropriate add-on selling offers and communications based on customer purchase histories. In creating customer databases for add-on selling, managers should remember that ideally they need individual purchase-behavior histories, generally available from a sales database. Many firms summarize individual purchase information; in doing so, they lose the capability to analyze cross-purchasing data. Instead, what is needed is a record of each transaction: products purchased, quantity purchased, purchase price, and date purchased.

Causal data are also critical in developing efficient and effective add-on selling strategies. A detailed description of a causal database can be found in chapter 3. Linking a causal database to individual purchase histories improves add-on selling by lowering add-on selling costs and increasing response rates. Costs are lowered because through analysis techniques the firm can identify and use tactics that are better suited to individual customers; the result is increased offer response rates.

### Accounting Metrics for Add-on Selling

Measuring the success of a firm's add-on selling strategy is central to managing customer equity. But what are the right measures to evaluate an add-on selling strategy? Successful add-on selling generally manifests itself through two basic metrics: changes in sales from retained customers, and changes in profits from retained customers.

The value of these metrics is to show whether the firm is growing sales effectively within its current base of customers or observing sales and profit changes because of customer acquisition. This can be determined by comparing changes in sales and profits from retained customers with changes in sales and profits overall. If sales or profits, or both, are decreasing from retained customers, the firm's add-on selling strategy may be ineffective and it may need to seek significant growth in new customers.

When computing changes in sales and profits over time, average sales and profit figures can be used. However, as measures, average sales and profits for retained customers have the same problem as the unadjusted retention rate. Specifically, these figures reflect the number of long- and short-life customers in the firm's database. Firms should therefore exercise caution and use duration-adjusted average sales and profit figures when examining changes in these metrics over time.

### *Analytical Tools for Add-on Selling*

Many types of analysis can be conducted to target customer and products for add-on selling. We explain three techniques in this section. The first, cross-buying analysis, focuses on determining which products have a high propensity to be purchased jointly. The second, collaborative filtering, matches customers who have similar purchasing profiles in order to identify appropriate products for add-on selling to specific customer types. The third, response modeling, uses statistical models (e.g., regression models and logit models) to estimate which customers are likely to respond to a new offering. All are valuable. The first helps to determine market communication strategies, the second to target potential customers with the right products, and the third to target customers in general. Table 5-6 summarizes the application of these tools to add-on selling.

**Table 5-6**
Application of Analytical Methods to Add-on Selling

| Analytical Method | Purpose | How It Improves Add-on Selling |
|---|---|---|
| Cross-purchase analysis; Log-linear models | Effectiveness | Determines which products are purchased together and hence which products to add-on sell |
| Collaborative filtering | Effectiveness | Identifies similar customers' buying behavior and hence which products to add-on sell |
| Logit/regression; Neural nets | Efficiency | Determines which customers to target |

## CROSS-BUYING ANALYSIS

Cross-buying analysis measures the likelihood of cross-buying between two products or services. It results in a measure that reflects the overall purchasing levels of the products analyzed. It is simple to compute and takes into account the two products' overall purchasing levels.

To begin, calculate the number of times that two products are purchased together as a percentage of a firm's total purchases. Let $Z_{ij}$ be the fraction of times that two products, $i$ and $j$, are purchased together. Next, compute the fraction of times product $i$ is purchased and the fraction of times product $j$ is purchased without the other; these values are denoted by $X_i$ and $X_j$, respectively. The cross-buying measure for products $i$ and $j$ is denoted by $CB_{ij}$.

$$CB_{ij} = Z_{ij} / (X_i \times X_j)$$

The theory of this measure is that if there is no relationship between the purchasing of $i$ and $j$, then the fraction of times that cross-buying will occur is simply $X_i \times X_j = Z_{ij}$. Therefore, if the ratio $CB_{ij}$ is greater than 1, there is cross-buying between the pair of products. If the ratio is significantly less than 1, the products have below-average cross-buying.

The concept and the calculation are simple. However, many firms do not use this calculation and therefore fail to adjust for the baseline percentage of times that products are purchased (that is, $X_i \times X_j$). Instead, when they find that two high-volume products are purchased together, they conclude that there is cross-buying. But this is not necessarily the case. The high incidence of joint purchasing may simply reflect the fact that each of the products is frequently purchased.

Consider the following application of cross-buying analysis. An Internet retailer wanted to utilize e-mail technology to enhance its add-on selling efficiency. It decided to mount a promotion campaign: Within four weeks of making a purchase from the site, a customer would receive a special targeted e-mail communication that promoted another add-on product. The challenge was determining which of the retailer's numerous products to feature in the promotion. This product choice was critical, because the better the appeal, the higher the likelihood that the customer would purchase the add-on and the higher the add-on selling profits would be. Of course, the most logical choice for an add-on is a product that is frequently purchased with the base product.

The retailer believed that there was a lot of cross-buying between the kitchenware category and the women's apparel category. Choosing one frequently purchased product from each category, the firm's analysts measured the fraction of all orders in which each product was purchased separately and the fraction of all orders in which the products were purchased jointly at one time. The result of this measurement produced a cross-buying ratio of 2.3. This suggested that the two items were frequently purchased together and that a communications campaign that encouraged buyers of one item to buy the other likely would have a good response rate.

## COLLABORATIVE FILTERING

Collaborative filtering is one of the most interesting techniques in advanced data analysis. It recognizes that if two customers purchase one set of similar products, then they are likely to buy other products in common as well. For example, if two customers each buy Bordeaux wines from certain vineyards and years, then if Customer A buys wine from another vineyard, Customer B is more likely to purchase wine from that other vineyard too.

Collaborative filtering is based on the assumption that similar purchasing implies similar tastes and interests. Amazon.com, for example, makes book recommendations to a customer based on both that customer's buying behavior and the buying behavior of other customers who have purchased the same or similar books.

Collaborative filtering improves effectiveness by enabling firms to make highly targeted offers. It helps firms to identify not only the appropriate categories for add-on selling but also appropriate items within categories.

## RESPONSE MODELING

Response modeling identifies those current customers most likely to respond to an offer. Its typical methods are regression analysis (e.g., the regression scoring models that were discussed in chapter 3) and logit models. These methods predict response to an add-on offer using a set of explanatory variables, such as recency, frequency, and monetary measures; marketing tactics implemented; and demographic and geographic data, if available.

Using the output from response models, managers can reduce the number of ads, sales calls, and other communications directed at customers with a low likelihood of buying. Using the models to score customers for each offer generally makes it possible to reduce selling expenses by 30 percent to 60 percent. This clearly improves efficiency of spending. Applying a response model to other prospective targets, firms can forecast response rates and thus increase the effectiveness of add-on selling tactics.

## Summary

Add-on selling offers a firm significant opportunity to enhance customer equity, but it must be managed carefully. It must be strategic, not just tactical. Too many firms use add-on selling as an opportunistic sales tool. But for add-on selling to reach its potential, a firm needs to develop a strategy that addresses issues such as managing affinity, using database marketing tools to increase efficiency and effectiveness, and outsourcing. With a solid strategy, a firm can determine how to maximize the return from its add-on selling opportunities. The idea of add-on selling is not new, but managing it effectively is more complex than simply trying to sell a customer one more product.

# 6

# OPTIMIZING
# CUSTOMER EQUITY

IN THEORY, the best way to optimize customer equity would be to maximize the profitability of each of its three main strategies: acquisition, retention, and add-on selling. In other words, allocate sufficient resources and pursue each strategy full steam ahead. However, practically speaking, most firms have limited resources; they cannot maximize the profitability of all three strategic initiatives simultaneously. Firms regularly must make resource-allocation decisions that involve trade-offs among their marketing strategies. The necessity for trade-offs demonstrates that customer equity can only be optimized through balance.

When one adds limitations on resources to the mix, it becomes clear that balance has strategic importance to the firm. However, the balancing dilemma is also revealed when firms assess their maximum thresholds for acquisition, retention, and add-on selling and where they stand relative to those thresholds. A firm that has a high retention rate already may be close to its maximum retention potential. Reaching, as opposed to being close to, this threshold may occur only at very high cost. Are the additional investments in retention worth it? Firms can address this issue only if they understand the need to look at all three strategies simultaneously and to trade off or balance their resource investments. The critical question for every marketing manager is, How should the firm optimize customer equity and allocate resources to each of these strategies simultaneously? Although a specific solution to this question will vary by firm, the best solutions will involve the development of an adaptive marketing system.

## An Adaptive Marketing System

An adaptive marketing system describes a customer-focused marketing process that places a high priority on developing customer knowledge and on implementing tactics that make use of it. The more information is available, the more the system adapts to accommodate the firm's customer needs. The value of a marketing program that is adaptive and built around the acquisition of customer knowledge is that the firm can leverage all aspects of the customer relationship when developing strategies and making trade-offs.

An area where adaptive marketing is commonly used is in Internet advertising. Advertising strategies on the Internet frequently involve the placement of multiple banner ads on several Web sites. Third-party ad servers monitor response rates (e.g., the click-through rate) to those ads and then refine both the placement and the ad selection based on advertising objectives and consumer response. Figure 6-1 displays this process pictorially. On the Internet, all of this can be done in minimal amounts of time. The end result is an advertisement campaign that enhances the client's customer equity and return on investment.

How does an adaptive marketing system allow firms to make a decision regarding balance? Figure 6-2 formally outlines an adaptive marketing system. Note that it describes a dynamic process. The dynamics are the key to the system's adaptability and its learning regarding customers. Another element contributing to the learning is the inputs from customer and behavioral or response data. It is the customer learning circulating through the system that facilitates refinements to the marketing mix. Customer equity is optimized as firms refine their marketing mix, thus creating a new strategic balance that is built on customer knowledge.

### Adjusting the Marketing Expenditures in an Adaptive Marketing System

Should a firm spend more on customers who are more responsive to expenditures or on those who are less responsive? In marketing, the

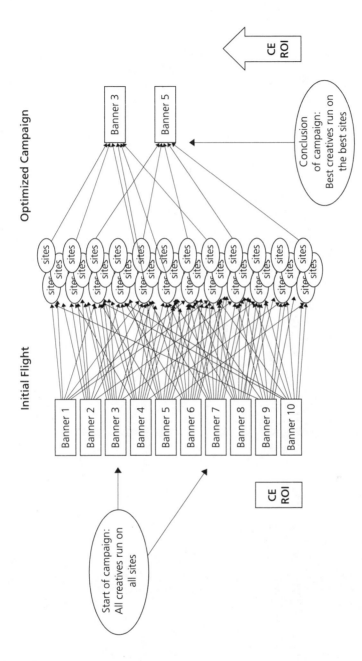

**Figure 6-1** Optimization Simulation

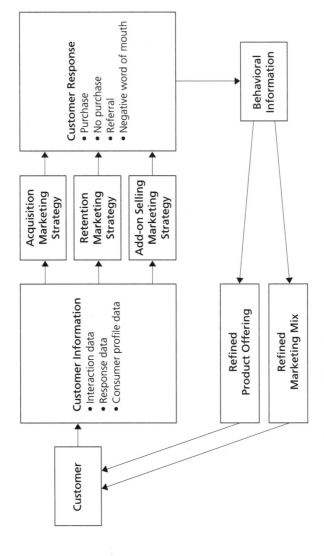

**Figure 6-2** Adaptive Marketing System

prevailing wisdom is "Invest in your best customers." However, less responsive customers may need encouragement to purchase, in the form of greater spending targeted at them. This suggests an alternative view: "Invest in your less responsive customers."

So which is it? Empirical analysis shows that when consumers are very sensitive to acquisition expenditures and less sensitive to retention expenditures, successful acquisition requires less investment than customer retention does.[1] This finding supports the logic behind investing in your less responsive customers. The basic principle becomes this: Direct more expenditures to areas in which consumers are less responsive.

Based on this principle, the next logical question is, In what situations might customers be less responsive or become less responsive to the firm's efforts and expenditures over time? Typically customers become less responsive as a product reaches the latter stages of the product life cycle. These stages often are characterized by high levels of customer knowledge about product options in the marketplace. As a result, many customers can and are willing to make purchase decisions based more on their experiences than on the firm's marketing tactics. In this situation, and counter to intuition, firms should increase their customer retention allocations. Ironically, firms do invest more in the later stages of the product life cycle, but through aggressive promotions or price cutting. These are actually retention investments.

How should the firm respond if a large part of its customer base is brand loyal? Brand-loyal customers tend to be very responsive to the firm's marketing expenditures and efforts. Therefore, from the research one could infer that the firm should shift expenditures away from retention and toward acquisition and add-on selling. By redirecting its expenditures this way, the firm increases the value of its entire base of customers by increasing its size (through acquisition) and its value (through add-on selling).

### Adjusting Pricing in an Adaptive Marketing System

One of the most difficult decisions a firm has to make is what price to charge customers over time. In chapter 4, which focused on retention strategy, we noted this key lesson: Short-term losses can translate into long-term gains. This lesson suggests that pricing should not aim to optimize transaction profitability. Rather, in keeping with the basic premise of customer equity, pricing over time should aim to optimize the customer's future value and dynamics. Having said that, we pose this question: When should the price of the first purchase be lower than the price of subsequent purchases, and vice versa?

Introductory and retention pricing can be observed in numerous situations. For example, magazines often offer one price for an initial subscription and a different price for a renewal subscription. In the credit card industry, firms offer special introductory interest rates or no annual fees for the first year. These examples represent a fairly common approach, in which the introductory price is lower than the subsequent renewal or retention price. However, although this is a common practice across numerous industries, no one has established that it is the optimal customer-management pricing strategy.

Researchers have found that, generally speaking, it is optimal for firms to increase prices over time.[2] This is an important finding, because it suggests that consumers with higher retention rates should *not* be offered lower prices. Instead, the firm can increase customer equity by increasing prices to its more loyal customers. This is consistent with the industry observation that loyal customers are *willing* to pay higher prices.[3] Switching costs, potential risks, and familiarity with a firm and its product are among the reasons that customers in longer customer–firm relationships are more willing to pay higher prices.

However, if customer price sensitivity increases over time, then a firm should lower its price over time. What causes price sensitivity to increase? A number of conditions characterize these situations. First, low switching costs can cause a customer to become more price sensitive. The second, related, factor is competition. As competition intensifies, there are more price offers to the customer. Third, customer preference can be flat or declining. In such conditions, a firm should lower its price.

Changes in a firm's cost structure also affect price. Suppose that the cost of providing a product or service decreases over time. Should the firm pass the savings on to customers, in the form of a price discount or a lower regular price? Research shows that if product costs decrease significantly over time, and if the firm seeks to manage the long-term value of its end users, then it is optimal for the firm to lower its prices over time. This research does not include recommendations on the optimal amount of the price reduction. However, it is likely that not all of the increased margin should get passed along to customers. Consumers seem to know this intuitively.

## Databases for an Adaptive Marketing System

An essential part of the learning in an adaptive marketing system is the customer and behavioral or response information. This is where customer databases enter the system. A firm's databases should include both prepurchase interaction data and postpurchase response data. Three basic premises should guide the collection of data to develop an adaptive marketing system:

1. Individual customer purchase behavior is essential in managing all aspects of customer equity to their potential.

2. Many customer–firm interactions do not relate directly to marketing, which means that a firm has to collect additional data beyond customer purchase data (e.g., customer service data) in order to manage customer equity.

3. Tracking marketing activities by customer significantly improves the efficiency and effectiveness of marketing programs. This in turn enhances customer equity.

The first premise implies that traditional marketing research information, which contributes to a general understanding of the customer, does not provide the specificity required for customer equity management. A firm needs to understand specific customer behavior, which it can track for lifetime value modeling and link to specific customer responses.

The second premise addresses the problem that many important customer interactions do not get measured. Inaccurate invoices and poor product delivery are examples of such interactions. Firms need to realize that all interactions, not just marketing communications and encounters, affect their customers' attitudes.

Finally, the third premise recognizes that causal data, with which firms can relate specific marketing actions to responses, are extremely valuable. With these data, firms can improve their acquisition, retention, and add-on selling strategies and implement tactics that are significantly more customer focused.

For example, a large European-owned apparel catalog company has developed a marketing system that adjusts its catalog based on the fashion orientation of each individual customer. Using the customer's purchases as a guide, the system determines his or her fashion orientation (e.g., fashion-forward, classic, conservative) and tailors the catalog's cover and sixteen inside pages to match. Each customer receives a unique catalog. The more often the customer purchases, the more accurately the firm can predict the fashion orientation and adapt its product offering and communications accordingly.

## Measuring Customer Equity

An adaptive system provides the environment for optimizing customer equity and achieving the appropriate strategic balance. Now let's see how to do it.

There are nine fundamental levers—three for each strategy—that a firm can manipulate to determine the appropriate balance that optimizes its customer equity. Those levers are acquisition rate ($Rate_{acq}$), acquisition margin per customer ($Margin_{acq}$), acquisition marketing expenditures per customer ($Expenditures_{acq}$), retention rate ($Rate_{ret}$), retention margin per customer ($Margin_{ret}$), retention marketing expenditures per customer ($Expenditures_{ret}$), add-on buying rate ($Rate_{a-o}$), add-on selling margin per customer ($Margin_{a-o}$), and marketing expenditures per customer for add-on selling ($Expenditures_{a-o}$). Using these levers we can compute customer equity. Figure 6-3 shows how the levers relate and are combined to forecast an expected value of customer equity per individual.[4] (For the purposes of demonstration we ignore the discounting of future cash flows.) This measure can be summed across individuals to obtain the equity of a firm's entire database of customers.

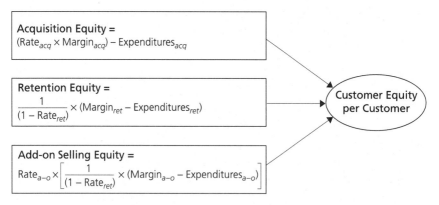

**Figure 6-3**   Computing Customer Equity

Consistent with the three customer equity strategies, figure 6-3 shows that customer equity per individual equals acquisition equity plus retention equity plus add-on selling equity. Several other features are notable in this computation. First, the profits from acquisition, retention, and add-on selling are all dependent on the success rate of the firm at that activity. This success rate is captured in the acquisition rate, retention rate, and add-on selling rate. To determine the expected acquisition margin, therefore, the acquisition margin that is generated once the customer is acquired needs to be multiplied by the acquisition rate. Acquisition marketing expenditures are incurred whether the individual is acquired or not; therefore, the acquisition marketing expenditures are *not* multiplied by the acquisition rate.

In the case of the retention equity, we can use the retention rate to determine the duration of the customer–firm relationship given that the customer is acquired. If we assume that the retention rate is constant over time, the expected relationship duration is simply 1/(1 – retention rate).[5] Knowing this duration, we can compute the total profits the firm will realize over that duration from the core product purchase. These profits constitute the firm's retention equity.

Because add-on buying generally occurs on repeat-purchase occasions, we will assume that the time horizon for add-on buying is the same as the duration of the retention phase of the relationship, that is, 1/(1 – retention rate). However, the add-on selling profits also depend on how successful the firm is at this endeavor. Therefore the expected add-on selling equity equals the add-on selling profits over the duration of the relationship times the add-on buying rate.

Implied in this example computation of customer equity are several assumptions:

1. Discounting of future profits is ignored. This can be easily rectified, however.

2. The margin and expenditures are constant over time. Once the firm knows the relationship duration, it is a simple task to adjust the margin each time period and sum up the profits each period using the new margins.

3. The customer retention rate does not change over time. This is the most critical assumption.

For firms whose customer churn rate is fairly constant, the third assumption is not a bad one. Others may want to relax this assumption to get a more precise prediction of their customer equity. When this assumption is relaxed, the issue of the appropriate time horizon to use in projecting retention rates into the future becomes critical. This issue, as well as others that may arise when refining a customer equity computation, is addressed later in this chapter.

Relaxing the retention rate assumption can refine the customer equity computation but requires more sophisticated modeling techniques, such as survival functions. More information about relaxing these assumptions and how more complex techniques can be applied to compute customer equity can be found on our Web site, www.customerequity.com. For the purpose of getting started, we stick with these assumptions here and provide an example of the complete computation in table 6-1.

A benefit of the way in which this computation is derived is that firms can easily see the drivers of their total customer equity. Another important insight can be seen by comparing the acquisition, retention, and add-on selling equities with the respective expenditures for each strategy. Given that firms often incur losses with customer acquisition, it is not uncommon for the acquisition equity to be negative while the acquisition marketing expenditures are a large proportion of the total marketing expenditures. It is idealistic but generally not realistic to expect that the percentage of total customer equity that is attributable to acquisition equity will equal the percentage of total marketing expenditures that are attributable to acquisition. The same holds true for retention and add-on selling. Regardless, firms should be aware of this comparison and monitor changes in these figures.

Suppose a firm that has a 70 percent retention rate and is close to its upper threshold on retention performed this computation and found that acquisition equity accounted for negative 10 percent of the firm's total customer equity, retention equity accounted for 50 percent, and add-on selling equity accounted for 60 percent. Looking at marketing expenditures in this light, the analysis revealed that 40 percent of the expenditures are directed toward acquisition, 40 percent toward retention, and 20 percent toward add-on selling. These figures show that although the firm spends heavily on acquisition, losses are generated that must be subsidized by other elements of the firm's strategy, such as add-on selling. Judging from the expenditures alone, the importance

**Table 6-1**

Example of Computing Customer Equity

| | | Percentage of Total |
|---|---|---|
| ACQUISITION EQUITY COMPUTATION | | |
| Acquisition rate | 6.00% | |
| Acquisition margin per customer per period | $960.00 | |
| Acquisition marketing expenditures per customer per period | $133.33 | 62.08 |
| Expected acquisition equity per customer lifetime | −$75.73 | −6.37 |
| RETENTION EQUITY COMPUTATION | | |
| Retention rate | 42.00% | |
| Retention margin per customer per period | $960.00 | |
| Retention marketing expenditures per customer per period | $71.43 | 33.26 |
| Expected retention equity per customer lifetime | $1,532.02 | 128.87 |
| ADD-ON SELLING EQUITY COMPUTATION | | |
| Add-on selling response rate | 18.00% | |
| Add-on selling margin per customer per period | $500.00 | |
| Add-on selling expenditures per customer per period | $10.00 | 4.66 |
| Expected add-on selling equity per customer lifetime | $155.16 | 13.05 |
| Total marketing expenditures per customer | $214.76 | |
| **Expected customer equity per customer** | **$1,188.82** | |

of add-on selling is not clear. However, the significant contribution of add-on selling equity shows its importance and suggests that maybe the firm could invest more heavily in this area and enhance its total customer equity. Investing more in retention is another option, although less desirable given that the firm is close to its maximum retention potential and that therefore incremental increases in retention may be costly.

## Using the Fundamental Levers to Optimize Customer Equity

Having computed the equity of an individual customer, the firm can change the values of the fundamental levers to see how total customer equity and individual component equities change. Changes in the levers are related to changes in the marketing strategy and tactics. For example, changes in the firm's pricing strategy should be reflected in both the success rate and the margin of a strategic component. Specifically, if a firm decreases its acquisition price, the acquisition rate is likely to increase and the transaction margins will decrease. Marketing expenditure changes (e.g., changes in customer service support) will also affect the success rate of a strategy. Mathematical formulas that vary in complexity can be used to link specific tactics to the rates. Some of these can be found on our Web site (www.customerequity.com). Although more subjective, managerial insight can also be used to approximate the relationship between a marketing mix change and the resulting change in the fundamental levers of the customer equity computation.

For the purposes of identifying a strategic balance that optimizes customer equity, sensitivity analysis is a first step in pointing the firm toward the right balance. Using the acquisition and retention data from table 6-1, table 6-2 shows an example of a sensitivity analysis that explores the impact of increasing marketing expenditures for add-on selling. Managerial judgment or statistical models can be used to approximate the impact that expenditure changes will have on the add-on purchasing rate.[6] In the example in table 6-2 we use managerial judgment to approximate retention rates.

When performing and drawing inferences from a sensitivity analysis, firms should consider the plausibility of a scenario. Can a firm increase its retention rate by 20 percent with only a 5 percent increase

**Table 6-2**
Example of Sensitivity Analysis

| Expected Customer Equity per Customer ($) | Expected Add-on Buying Rate (%) | Add-on Expenditures ($) | % Change in CE |
|---|---|---|---|
| 1,188.82 | 18 | 10.00 | |
| 1,206.06 | 20 | 10.50 | 1 |
| 1,240.54 | 24 | 10.75 | 4 |
| 1,275.02 | 28 | 11.00 | 7 |
| 1,292.26 | 30 | 11.10 | 9 |

*Note:* For demonstration purposes only, this analysis assumes that the retention rate will not be affected by additional add-on purchases.

in retention marketing expenditures? Scenarios that exceed the firm's upper and lower thresholds for rates, margins, and expenditures should not be considered.

Although managerial judgment is always needed in arriving at a balance decision, the most rigorous and objective method for determining a strategic balance involves using constrained optimization techniques. The Solver tool in Microsoft Excel performs this type of analysis.

To see the importance and roles of managerial judgment, the fundamental levers of optimization, and data analysis in the balance and optimization decision, consider the following case study. The names and company profiles in this example are fictional and represent an amalgam of firms.

## Case Study: Balancing Customer Equity Strategies

Donelson & Ward is a venerable manufacturing company in the Northeastern region of the United States. It has been in business since the 1920s. Its primary products are hoses and fittings designed for agricultural, mining, automotive, and aerospace applications. In 1996 Donelson & Ward had a customer base of approximately 5,300 direct customers and 500 distributors worldwide.

The company's CEO, Sally Donelson, had been reading extensively about customer loyalty and retention, and she decided to convene a meeting with her top management. Ms. Donelson had decided that they should embark on a major investment in customer service improvements by adding customer service representatives who would work with customers after they were acquired. The goal was to increase retention rates and sales per customer. However, Ms. Donelson was having difficulty determining if the investment would pay out. All of the customer retention and loyalty books implied that higher loyalty was a good thing (who could disagree with that?), but they failed to discuss the financial trade-offs of changing retention rates.

To prepare for the meeting, Ms. Donelson hired a consulting firm, BCA, to help her evaluate whether her investment in customer service made sense. If she made the investment, she also would want measures put in place that would indicate whether the investment was continuing to pay out. A lead partner at BCA, Tom Harris, began by obtaining customer and financial data from the company.

The financial data Mr. Harris obtained showed that sales and profits for Donelson & Ward increased by about 2.6 percent and 38.3 percent, respectively, in 1996, as shown in table 6-3. Donelson & Ward had taken cost out of its product, which resulted in a hefty boost to profits.

With the customer data collected, Mr. Harris began to determine the current state of Donelson & Ward's customer value. Table 6-4 shows retention rates, sales, and margins for cohorts of customers who began a relationship with the firm in 1990. Mr. Harris then developed a set of measures to show how the customer base had changed from 1994 to 1996. These measures appear in table 6-5.

The results from these tables create an interesting picture. Although the firm has been growing sales, most of the growth has come from existing customers as they have matured. Average retention rates,

**Table 6-3**
Sales and Profits for Donelson & Ward

| Year | Number of Customers | Sales ($) | Gross Margin ($) | General Administrative and Selling Expense ($) | Pretax Profits ($) |
|------|------|------|------|------|------|
| 1994 | 5,258 | 369,201,436 | 98,441,103 | 81,224,316 | 17,216,787 |
| 1995 | 5,441 | 387,496, 292 | 106,124,943 | 85,249,184 | 20,875,758 |
| 1996 | 5,309 | 397,577,560 | 117,522,450 | 88,659,796 | 28,862,654 |

**Table 6-4**
Sales, Gross Margins, and Retention Rates for Customers Acquired in 1990

| Year | Sales in Period ($) | Gross Margin (%) | Gross Margin ($) | Retention Rate (%) |
|------|------|------|------|------|
| 1990 | 30,000 | 30.0 | 9,000 | 50.0 |
| 1991 | 75,000 | 35.0 | 26,250 | 60.0 |
| 1992 | 85,000 | 35.0 | 29,750 | 75.0 |
| 1993 | 100,000 | 40.0 | 40,000 | 85.0 |
| 1994 | 100,000 | 40.0 | 40,000 | 90.0 |
| 1995 | 100,000 | 40.0 | 40,000 | 95.0 |
| 1996 | 100,000 | 40.0 | 40,000 | 95.0 |

**Table 6-5**
Traditional Customer Measures

| Year | Number of Customers Acquired | Total Number of Customers | Retention Rate (%) | Average Sales per Customer ($) |
|------|------------------------------|---------------------------|--------------------|--------------------------------|
| 1994 | 1,800 | 5,258 | 68.41 | 70,217 |
| 1995 | 1,800 | 5,441 | 69.25 | 71,218 |
| 1996 | 1,500 | 5,309 | 70.01 | 74,884 |

at approximately 70 percent, appear to be good. However, the total number of customers actually declined between 1995 and 1996.

Based on his analysis, Mr. Harris recommended that Donelson & Ward concentrate on acquisition while maintaining their current retention rates. Ms. Donelson, who believed higher retention rates would drive the long-term success of the firm, did not greet this recommendation kindly.

### One Year Later

In spite of the compelling argument made by Mr. Harris, Donelson & Ward decided to add customer service representatives and to decrease customers per salesperson. Ms. Donelson was mesmerized by the appeal of higher retention rates that had been so heavily touted in the popular business press.

In the year since the customer service representatives were added, sales grew at a slow rate while profits actually decreased. Ms. Donelson recognized that the addition of sales and customer service representatives would add to short-term costs, but she was surprised at the decrease in profitability and was particularly concerned about the lack of sales growth. Mr. Harris was asked to analyze what impact the sales and customer service changes had on Donelson & Ward's business.

Mr. Harris decided to use customer equity accounting measures to diagnose how the underlying dynamic structure of the customer base had changed. The measures are given in table 6-6. A perusal of this table shows that new customer acquisitions had declined significantly in 1996 and remained at that low point. Therefore, if per-customer acquisition costs remained the same, the firm's acquisition equity (i.e., the expected profit from these new customers) would be much lower in the future. Mr. Harris also noted that sales in 1997 had risen because customers who were acquired from 1994 to 1996 were now more mature

**Table 6-6**
Customer Equity Accounting Measures

| Year | Number of Customers Acquired | New Customer Investment ($) | New Customer Investment as a Percentage of Sales (%) | Duration-Adjusted Retention Rates (%) | Duration-Adjusted Add-on Sales ($) |
|---|---|---|---|---|---|
| 1994 | 1,800 | 27,990,000 | 7.58 | 76.1 | 80,748 |
| 1995 | 1,800 | 27,990,000 | 7.22 | 76.1 | 80,748 |
| 1996 | 1,500 | 23,325,000 | 5.87 | 77.9 | 84,601 |
| 1997 | 1,500 | 23,325,000 | 5.68 | 77.9 | 84,601 |

and their sales levels had increased. However, he anticipated that future sales growth would decline due to the declining trend in acquisitions.

As far as retention was concerned, Mr. Harris found that retention rates had remained static despite the emphasis on customer service representatives. He used a duration-adjusted retention rate (discussed in chapter 4) and found that the retention rate stayed at 77.9 percent. Note that this is different from the average retention rates used in table 6-5.

Mr. Harris presented his results to Ms. Donelson. She was surprised. The most disturbing fact to her was that new-customer investment (i.e., expenditures aimed at acquiring new customers) was declining. After further investigation, she found that adding customer service representatives had actually decreased the customer's contact with the sales force. The service representatives were readily available and therefore handled most of the client relationships. However, they were ineffective at both new customer sales and add-on sales. Although in the short run sales and profits had increased, the lack of new customer acquisition was going to hurt Donelson & Ward's long-term profitability and sales growth. Mr. Harris reiterated that Donelson & Ward already had good retention rates and that it should focus on acquiring new customers.

For the first time Ms. Donelson began to think that although retention is important, so is acquisition. Mr. Harris emphasized to Ms. Donelson that she should not construe his comments to mean that high retention rates are not important. They are. But in her case, so were acquisition and add-on selling. Through the measures he showed her, she began to recognize that she should restructure her organization to emphasize acquisition and add-on selling.

To overcome the company's problems, Ms. Donelson separated her sales organization into acquisition teams and add-on selling teams. Customer service representatives retained their retention role. Each sales and customer service organization was then compensated on how well it met its goals. Mr. Harris was convinced this would greatly improve Donelson & Ward's performance.

### What Happened?

After their last meeting, Ms. Donelson asked Mr. Harris to put together a pro forma income statement for an alternative strategy, one in which Donelson & Ward concentrated on customer acquisition as opposed to customer service and customer retention.

To demonstrate the impact of a customer-acquisition emphasis, Mr. Harris decided to assume 1,800 new customers each year (as opposed to the current 1,500 per year), beginning in 1998 and going through the year 2005. He then built a pro forma income statement, shown in tables 6-7 and 6-8, which reflects both acquisition strategies and the retention pattern of Donelson & Ward's customer base over time. Table 6-7 makes its projections based on 1,500 new customers per year;[7] table 6-8 assumes 1,800 new customers per year.

A comparison of the two strategies' results indicates that profits, discounted at a rate of 11.3 percent (Donelson & Ward's cost of capital), are greater for the increased-acquisition strategy after 2001. The statement also shows that the number of customers at the end of 2005 comes to 7,275 for the increased-acquisition strategy versus 6,319 for the base case. Although this statistic is not included in the typical pro forma calculation of business decisions, it is important in a customer equity analysis.

We can quantify the impact of having a much larger customer base in 2005 by approximating the customer equity value of the customer base for both decisions. Tables 6-7 and 6-8 show that discounted customer value in 2005 is $980,736,363 under the base acquisition strategy, whereas it is $1,129,121,047 under the increased-acquisition strategy. This is a significant increase in customer equity, and it results from the shift in emphasis from retention to acquisition. Unfortunately, because typical pro forma customer-investing computations do not account for the terminal value of the customer base, senior management may decide not to invest in customer growth. Furthermore, because firms do not show the sizes of their customer bases, analysts

**Table 6-7**
Customer Valuation for Donelson & Ward: Base Acquisition

| Year | Number of Customers | Sales ($) | Gross Margin ($) | General Administrative and Selling Expense ($) | Pretax Profits ($) | NPV of Customer ($) | Estimated Value of Customer ($) | Ratio of Value of Customer Base to Pretax Profits | Discounted Value of Customer Base ($) | Discounted Pretax Profits ($) |
|---|---|---|---|---|---|---|---|---|---|---|
| 1998 | 5,442 | 417,127,062 | 124,536,188 | 93,019,335 | 31,516,853 | 295,039 | 1,605,481,950 | 50.94 | | |
| 1999 | 5,567 | 430,884,743 | 128,864,817 | 96,087,298 | 32,777,519 | 295,039 | 1,642,380,493 | 50.11 | 1,642,380,493 | 32,777,519 |
| 2000 | 5,702 | 446,421,045 | 134,289,588 | 99,551,893 | 34,737,695 | 295,039 | 1,682,182,212 | 48.43 | 1,511,394,620 | 31,210,867 |
| 2001 | 5,834 | 461,473,053 | 139,633,366 | 102,908,491 | 36,724,875 | 295,039 | 1,721,279,453 | 46.87 | 1,389,508,014 | 29,646,266 |
| 2002 | 5,963 | 475,997,925 | 144,833,992 | 106,147,537 | 38,686,455 | 295,039 | 1,759,246,405 | 45.47 | 1,275,972,103 | 28,059,081 |
| 2003 | 6,087 | 489,970,129 | 149,874,484 | 109,263,339 | 40,611,145 | 295,039 | 1,795,973,744 | 44.22 | 1,170,359,611 | 26,464,554 |
| 2004 | 6,207 | 503,372,948 | 154,742,060 | 112,252,167 | 42,489,892 | 295,039 | 1,831,380,863 | 43.10 | 1,072,266,777 | 24,877,676 |
| 2005 | 6,319 | 515,831,195 | 159,281,163 | 115,030,357 | 44,250,806 | 295,039 | 1,864,332,043 | 42.13 | 980,736,363 | 23,278,243 |

**Table 6-8**
Customer Valuation for Donelson & Ward: Increased-Acquisition Strategy

| Year | Number of Customers | Sales ($) | Gross Margin ($) | General Administrative and Selling Expense ($) | Pretax Profits ($) | NPV of Customer ($) | Estimated Value of Customer ($) | Ratio of Value of Customer Base to Pretax Profits | Discounted Value of Customer Base ($) | Discounted Pretax Profits ($) |
|---|---|---|---|---|---|---|---|---|---|---|
| 1998 | 5,907 | 439,570,812 | 124,419,001 | 98,024,291 | 26,394,710 | 295,039 | 1,742,675,316 | 66.02 | | 28,814,920 |
| 1999 | 6,134 | 462,458,768 | 131,943,226 | 103,128,305 | 28,814,920 | 295,039 | 1,809,756,400 | 62.81 | 1,809,756,400 | 28,814,920 |
| 2000 | 6,351 | 486,588,270 | 140,805,276 | 108,509,184 | 32,296,092 | 295,039 | 1,873,704,151 | 58.02 | 1,683,471,834 | 29,017,154 |
| 2001 | 6,555 | 509,202,294 | 149,173,861 | 113,552,111 | 35,621,749 | 295,039 | 1,934,049,901 | 54.29 | 1,561,267,598 | 28,755,764 |
| 2002 | 6,750 | 530,684,220 | 157,157,309 | 118,342,581 | 38,814,728 | 295,039 | 1,991,565,481 | 51.31 | 1,444,471,899 | 28,152,117 |
| 2003 | 6,936 | 551,056,916 | 164,757,997 | 122,885,692 | 41,872,305 | 295,039 | 2,046,277,557 | 48.87 | 1,333,471,948 | 27,286,398 |
| 2004 | 7,112 | 570,348,185 | 171,980,954 | 127,187,645 | 44,793,308 | 295,039 | 2,098,230,635 | 46.84 | 1,228,506,340 | 26,226,318 |
| 2005 | 7,275 | 588,223,808 | 178,687,006 | 131,173,909 | 47,513,097 | 295,039 | 2,146,404,097 | 45.17 | 1,129,121,047 | 24,994,379 |

likely cannot evaluate them on the basis of their customer-growth strategies.

With the numbers from his analysis, Mr. Harris convinced Ms. Donelson that at the end of 2005, the firm would be far more valuable to shareholders if it invested in the increased customer acquisition strategy.

## Summary

As the case study shows, achieving the right strategic balance is not an easy task. Many factors play roles in the allocation decision. However, looking at customer equity by analyzing each individual equity component can assist in diagnosing the drivers of customer equity and analyzing opportunities for enhancement. Running a sensitivity analysis to see how customer equity changes as one or several of the levers change can provide managers with needed insight to achieve a balanced effort.

# PART III

---

# MANAGING BY CUSTOMER EQUITY

# 7

# THE MARKETING MIX

THIS CHAPTER is where the rubber meets the road. For customer equity management to assist managers, it is essential that it lead to tactics that are different from typical brand marketing.

The traditional approaches to marketing strategy and tactics revolve around STP—segmentation, targeting, and positioning. This brand-driven approach to marketing strategy works well with products and services for which the major issue is branding or making some product modifications (i.e., slight changes in the attributes can allow the firm to reposition the product). Advertising agencies thrive on STP. This is their paradigm, although it is generally dressed up in a more sophisticated way. This approach is fundamentally about determining the target audience and then pounding away at the brand's positioning with a barrage of advertisements in print and electronic media.

Customer equity is driven by a different paradigm, the ARA (acquisition, retention, and add-on selling) model of marketing. Given this model, there are two critical issues that influence the marketing mix decision: the individual's stage in the customer life cycle, and industry thresholds for acquisition, retention, and add-on selling.

## Marketing Strategy and Tactics by Stage in the Life Cycle

Different marketing strategies and tactics apply at various stages of the customer life cycle. To most effectively manage customer equity, firms must be able to identify customers at different stages of the life cycle and be willing and able to market to them differently. In this discussion we focus on six elements of the marketing mix: advertising, sales force efforts, pricing, promotion, product or service offering, and customer service. Table 7-1 summarizes how different elements of the marketing mix can influence each component of the ARA model of customer equity. Table 7-2 summarizes the approach to take in each of these areas at each stage of the customer life cycle.

### *Prospects*

The prospect stage presents two major marketing problems: making the prospect aware of the firm's products or services, and inducing an initial purchase. To address the first problem, marketers can use advertising and other communication tools to position the product and to generate awareness. (Prospects require the highest advertising investment because they are the least likely to know about the product.) The sales force can generate awareness as well by calling on prospects directly and communicating the product's value. In many industries the sales force devotes its most intense effort to wooing prospects.

Once product awareness exists, the company needs to convince potential customers to try the product. Tools used to generate initial purchases include promotions, such as discounts off list prices, and the concentration of sales efforts on the company's lead product or service. It is common to offer price discounts to generate the initial trial of products that customers repurchase frequently, and companies selling industrial products often offer lower introductory prices to compensate potential customers for switching costs and the perceived risks of using a new supplier.

At the prospect stage, firms should concentrate on lead products: basic products the customer can buy that eventually lead to trade-ups and add-on selling. The sales force generally should focus on selling this product to prospective customers. Later, sales of related and premium products will evolve.

At this stage, customer service does not play a very prominent role, because the prospect has yet to make any purchases. However, initial

**Table 7-1**
How Marketing Mix Affects Components of Customer Equity

| Element of the Marketing Mix | Acquisition | Retention | Add-on Selling | General Comments |
|---|---|---|---|---|
| Advertising Copy | Awareness | Direct customer communication | Affinity with the firm; targeted communications regarding offers | Primary use of advertising copy is awareness generation and creation of customer affinity |
| Media selection | Mass media cost-effective | Database marketing | Database marketing | Once the customer has purchased, the firm creates a database to develop targeted communications |
| Customer service | Affects word-of-mouth communications | A primary vehicle for creating high retention levels | Increases response rates for add-on offers | Primary vehicle for retention and can significantly affect add-on selling response |
| Product quality | Affects word-of-mouth | Product reliability creates high retention levels | Increases response rates for add-on offers | Has similar effect as customer service, but high product reliability decreases need for customer service |
| Product positioning | Affects the size of the target market; creates customer expectations | High retention rates occur when positioning and delivery of product benefits match | Creates affinity with customer base, which increases add-on selling response | Positioning influences expectations, which will influence retention rates and the appeal of a product to potential new customers |

*(continued)*

**Table 7-1 (continued)**
How Marketing Mix Affects Components of Customer Equity

| Element of the Marketing Mix | Acquisition | Retention | Add-on Selling | General Comments |
|---|---|---|---|---|
| Promotions | Generates trial among potential customers | Can increase retention when unique rewards are offered to best customers | Increases response rates to add-on selling offers | Promotions are a form of reduced price and primarily increase acquisition rate and add-on selling response rates but can also increase retention rates if used properly |
| Channels of distribution | Third-party channels can increase customer acquisition | Third-party channels decrease retention rates because the channel owns the customer | Direct channel makes it easier to target third-party customers | Third-party channel (versus direct) increases ease of buying the product, which increases acquisition but decreases retention because the firm loses control of the customer |

**Table 7-2**
Marketing Mix by Stage in the Customer Life Cycle

|  | Prospects | First-Time Buyers | Early Repeat Buyers | Core Customers | Defectors |
|---|---|---|---|---|---|
| Advertising | Awareness | Reinforcement | Reinforcement | Personal | Apology |
| Sales Force | Closers | Personal service | Personal service | Personal service | Closers; personal service |
| Pricing | Low | Moderate | Increasing | Higher | Higher |
| Promotions | Trial | Similar to trial | Limited | Reward | Apology |
| Product Offerings | Lead | Second lead | Add-on | Add-on | Broad |
| Customer Service | Limited | Problem-focused | Problem-focused | Personal attention | Problem-focused |

contacts with the company, such as interactions with sales staff, will give the prospect expectations of what future customer service will—or should—be like.

### First-time Buyers

First-time buyers are customers in the trial stage. They have made a purchase but are still evaluating the firm and the product. The strategy at this stage should have two objectives: to reinforce the customer's belief that the firm's products are superior and to induce a second purchase. Advertising and customer service both contribute to the former.

Advertising reinforces the new customer's decision to buy, and its message should emphasize the product's value and benefits. The demands on customer service can vary among industries. In some, customers require extensive service just to start using a product. They may need help with installation, training, or integration of the product into other systems. The quality of this service plays a critical role in reinforcing the purchase decision. In others, product problems can occur. If a personal computer or a washing machine does not work properly, the customer often knows soon after plugging it in. First-time buyers in this situation require excellent customer service before they will consider buying again from the same company.

If not the same lead product, the product offering at this stage should be a second lead product—another product that is easy for the customer to buy. Promotions need to induce repeat purchasing without hurting the product's image. Aggressive promotions at this stage may cause the customer to develop a low reference price for the product. This would result in long-term price discounting. Pricing, although important, is less critical at this stage as long as the product offered provides good value to the customer.

### Early Repeat Buyers

Early repeat customers are less vulnerable than first-time customers. They have made several purchases and have signaled their interest in the firm's products. They also have indicated that the current value provided by the firm's products is acceptable; pricing does not play a major role as long as it is competitive.

Nonetheless, these are not core customers. Three factors can cause early repeat buyers to defect: customer service problems, product performance problems, or superior products from competitors. To prevent defections for these reasons, the firm should provide excellent customer service to this group. If competitors introduce a superior product, the firm should lower its price to early repeat buyers in recognition of their value in the long run.

Promotions do not play a large role for this customer segment. Any that are used should focus on making these customers more routine buyers. Product offerings should consist of add-on products that complement or are related to the firm's core products. Likewise, advertising is not critical to these customers, but some communications should convey the firm's appreciation for their business.

## Core Customers

Core customers—the firm's most highly valued customers—are critical to overall profitability. The firm must develop aggressive strategies to keep them on board.

Promotions should be used to signal to core customers their importance and value. Reward systems can accomplish this very effectively. Pricing for this consumer segment is very complex. A firm's best customers commonly end up paying higher average prices than its new customers do. This does not appear to make sense, but there is a rationale behind it. Core customers often have higher switching costs. They also have greater knowledge of the firm's products and can recognize the superior value these products provide. For both these reasons, core customers will bear higher prices than prospects will.

Offering higher prices to core customers carries risks, as in the example of Internet service providers (ISPs). In the ISP case the most profitable customers have learned the advantages of frequently switching in pursuit of low introductory charges. In response, many ISPs have had to lower their rates to existing customers as well.

The sales force's goal regarding core customers should be to provide superior customer service and to identify quickly any problems these customers might have. As a general rule, advertising and other marketing communications should take advantage of any available customer information. Core customers should receive product information relevant to their historical buying patterns.

## Defectors

Defectors are core customers who for some reason have decided to stop doing business with the company. Sometimes external events cause their defection. In that case, there is nothing the firm can do to reinstate them. Some defectors, however, are salvageable, and their high potential customer equity makes them worth a strong effort. Again, because defectors were highly valuable customers before and could be again, the firm can afford to make a significant investment in their return.

A marketing strategy designed to woo back a defector usually begins with an understanding of why the customer defected in the first place. To do this, a firm may find that, given the defector's high potential financial value, it pays to invest in personal contact with the customer. Once the problem is identified—perhaps the customer received a faulty product or the service fell short of expectations—the firm can develop a personal selling solution to overcome the problem. This solution may include an "apology reward" (an apology for the error along with a free offer), a personal visit, or special pricing.

Although firms can adopt a marketing mix strategy that is appropriate for different stages in the customer life cycle, they still may be limited by industry thresholds for acquisition, retention, and add-on selling. The next section describes how firms can overcome these limitations.

## Marketing Strategy to Influence Industry Thresholds for the Components of Customer Equity

Throughout this book we refer to upper thresholds or maximum levels of acquisition, retention, and offer response for an industry. If the firm spends an infinite amount on acquisition spending, the maximum acquisition response will be a number far less than 1. The reason is that no matter how much a firm spends, a large segment of customers will not purchase the product or service. Suppose Merrill Lynch buys a large amount of television advertising time for its financial consulting services to individual investors. There are many consumers who will not use it because they do not need the service. Even if the service were free, they would not use it. Only if Merrill Lynch offered free stock in a given company would they have a high sign-up rate, and even then they would not acquire 100 percent of the population because some perspective customers would be leery of the offer.

For each component of customer equity there is a maximum level. Retention is constrained because of the natural turnover rate in an industry and changes in consumer preferences; add-on selling is constrained because of the limited need for a specific new product or service offered.

Most firms are unaware of the drivers of the industry thresholds and do not know how to change them. Without knowing these drivers, firms are less effective at employing the marketing mix to change them and increase customer equity. Federal Express is an example of a firm that understood the drivers of customer equity in its industry; with that knowledge it changed the maximum retention level in its industry.

### The Federal Express Story

As has been recounted many times, Federal Express changed the air delivery service industry. Prior to Federal Express's entry, air delivery firms would use the scheduled airlines to move packages from point A to B. They were dependent on the airlines' schedules and on-time records. Even back in the mid-1970s, airlines had delays and cancellation problems—not as severe as in 2000, but enough to cause serious reliability problems for the air delivery service companies. The typical on-time record for a delivery service was 43 percent. This obviously led to enormous customer dissatisfaction and low retention rates. Customers were constantly changing their air freight delivery company.

Federal Express recognized this problem and decided to change the structure of how air freight was handled. In other words, they developed a marketing mix strategy that focused on distribution and was unique to the industry. They introduced the idea of a central hub (Memphis) to which all packages came and were then routed to their final destination. As important, they also purchased their own fleet of planes, which eliminated the dependency on the scheduled airlines. They flew planes at night, which meant airport delays were minimal. This strategy allowed Federal Express to create their now famous slogan: "When it absolutely, positively has to be there overnight." Federal Express's retention rate became significantly higher than the industry average (percentages in the 90s versus 43 percent), and in time they became the market leader.

Federal Express changed the industry maximum retention rate through a totally new strategy for logistics and operation that they then marketed through their famous advertising campaigns.

### Acquisition Thresholds

The primary determinants of maximum levels for acquisition response rates are the stage of the industry in its product life cycle, industry innovation, purchase frequency, and switching level (low retention rates).

- *Stage in the product life cycle:* The general rule is that the acquisition threshold is highest during the growth stage of the product life cycle, declines as the product matures, and ebbs as the product life cycle reaches the decline phase.

- *Industry innovation:* Generally, the greater the innovation in an industry, the more reason customers have to change suppliers. This leads to new customers being acquired. The personal computer market is a good example. As the technology keeps changing, both firms and consumers search for the best supplier of the new technology.

- *Purchase frequency:* As a guideline, the shorter the purchase frequency, the greater the number of opportunities to switch suppliers. Industries with products with short purchase frequency will have far greater overall acquisition rates (due to switching) than do industries with long purchase frequency.

- *Low industry retention:* Low retention rates in an industry obviously generate higher acquisition baseline rates.

## CHANGING THRESHOLDS ON ACQUISITION RATES

Once a firm understands the determinants of the maximum acquisition rate, it is necessary to develop a strategy to increase that rate. Changing industry thresholds is a significant endeavor. It requires a one-time expenditure or a process change. It is important to distinguish this effort from increasing per-period expenditures. Per-period expenditures affect how rapidly the firm reaches the upper threshold, not the overall level.

Methods to increase the threshold level are as follows: new industry positioning, increasing the market size, and increasing awareness. Marketing communications, sales force, and distribution can all play a role in these changes.

An example is $H_2$ blockers (e.g., Zantac and Pepcid). The Federal Drug Administration allowed pharmaceutical companies to market the product over the counter, no longer requiring prescriptions. This opened up a vast segment of the U.S. population to the producers of $H_2$ blockers. The result was that the maximum acquisition level increased exponentially.

## *Retention Thresholds*

Changing maximum retention rates has been the focus of most of the customer relationship management (CRM) literature. The CRM literature does not describe its objective as changing baseline retention rates, but in actuality that is the focus. Articles and books explain how a firm can make one-time investments to develop contact strategies, improve customer service, and affect the culture of the organization, each of which affects the maximum retention rate.

Three commonly used mechanisms to change retention thresholds are improving product or service reliability, improving product or service quality without increasing price, and introducing new products or services.

### IMPROVING PRODUCT OR SERVICE RELIABILITY

An example of a process change to improve reliability and service is provided by Southwest Airlines. Through a different operational model they provide customers with a much better on-time record and fewer cancelled flights than the traditional service-oriented carriers. They do it through the use of one type of aircraft, no interairline ticketing, no seat assignments, and no meals. While Southwest's service to the customer is minimal in terms of the accoutrements of flying, they are always close to the top of the industry in customer satisfaction. As stated, they do it through simplified systems, which is a one-time investment and does not increase operating costs.

### IMPROVING PRODUCT OR SERVICE QUALITY WITHOUT INCREASING PRICE

It is easy to recommend improving product or service quality without increasing price. If it is feasible and successful, it is a winning strategy. But how can a firm accomplish this objective? The usual mechanism for making these improvements is technology. For example, Federal Express's Internet package tracking improves service without increasing the price to the customer.

### DEVELOPING NEW PRODUCTS OR SERVICES

Developing new products or services is an obvious strategy, but again is difficult to implement. An example is provided by Intel. It is in a highly competitive industry (chip design and manufacturing); if it is not able to continually innovate with new products, it will lose its market share. R&D is essential to maintaining loyal customers. When AMD, one of its direct competitors, was able to produce a faster chip than Intel, Intel matched it almost immediately. Because the customer wants faster megahertz, it is necessary to continually innovate.

### Add-on Selling Thresholds

The primary determinants affecting the upper limits of responses to add-on selling are the size of the market, the affinity the customer has with the firm, and how cost-effective the firm is in making offers.

EXPANDING THE MARKET SIZE

Trying to increase the size of the market through a one-time investment versus ongoing marketing costs requires repositioning the firm's product lines to fit new markets. This generally requires some product modifications, not simply a sophisticated advertising campaign. As an example, a traditional bank broadened its product lines to include insurance, discount brokerage, and other services to transform it into a one-stop financial services firm. Brokerage houses began offering loans and other types of financial instruments. Each broadened its market appeal.

AFFINITY

Influencing customer affinity requires rethinking the business or businesses the firm is in (a one-time decision). Because of this we have classified it as a mechanism that changes the maximum response potential to add-on selling offers. Customer affinity is discussed extensively in chapter 5 and will not be repeated here.

COST EFFECTIVENESS OF MAKING OFFERS

Database marketing and sophisticated statistical methods allow firms to drive down the costs of making offers by matching customers with the appropriate products. This then increases the number of offers that can be made for the same cost, hence increasing the maximum add-on selling rates.

In summary, there are a significant number of business strategies and tactics that can be used to affect the industry thresholds for acquisition, retention, and add-on selling. A firm must recognize these possibilities and develop actionable, cost-effective plans to capitalize on them. If successful, they generally give the firm a strategic advantage (e.g., Federal Express), which then requires a significant investment for competition to replicate.

## Summary

The ARA model of customer equity requires a new approach to making the marketing mix decision. Tables 7-3 to 7-5 summarize how different elements of the marketing mix affect each component of acquisition, retention, and add-on selling. These tables are designed to help the reader understand at a glance how different marketing tactics change customer equity.

It is important to realize that the marketing mix decision is not a static decision. It should vary as customers evolve through different stages of the customer life cycle. Firms can proactively affect their success at the different stages by understanding the drivers of the thresholds to acquisition, retention, and add-on selling.

**Table 7-3**
Links between Acquisition and Marketing Mix

| Marketing Mix Variable | Acquisition Probability $(\alpha)$ | Acquisition Efficiency $(\lambda)$ | Size of Market $(N)$ |
|---|---|---|---|
| Advertising | | | |
|   Awareness | X | | X |
|   Positioning/Expectations | X | | X |
| Word of mouth | X | | |
| Segmentation/Targeting | X | X | X |
| Pricing | X | | |
| Promotions | X | | |
| Product quality | | | |
|   Quality | X | | |
|   Type | X | | X |
| Channel of distribution | X | X | X |
| Sales force | X | X | |
| Database marketing | | X | |

**Table 7-4**
Links between Retention and Marketing Mix

| Marketing Mix Variable | Retention Rate (ρ) | Retention Spending (B$_r$) | Retention Efficiency (γ) |
|---|---|---|---|
| Advertising | | | |
|   Awareness | | X | |
|   Positioning | X | | |
| Word of mouth | X | X | X |
| Segmentation/Targeting | X | X | X |
| Pricing/Value | X | | |
| Promotions | X | | |
| Product quality | | | |
|   Quality vs expectations | X | | |
|   Type | | X | |
| Channel of distribution | | X | X |
| Sales force | | X | X |
| Database marketing | X | X | X |

**Table 7-5**
Linking Add-on Selling and Marketing Mix

| Marketing Mix Variable | Add-on Selling Expenditure (B) | Number of Offers (J) | Response Rate per Offer (r) |
|---|---|---|---|
| Advertising | | | |
|   Awareness | | | |
|   Affinity | | X | |
| Word of mouth | | | X |
| Segmentation/Targeting | X | X | X |
| Pricing | | | X |
| Promotions | | | X |
| Product quality | | | X |
|   Quality | | | X |
|   Type | X | X | |
| Channel of distribution | X | | X |
| Sales force | | | X |
| Database marketing | X | X | X |

# 8

# Customer Equity
## Accounting

T HE MEASURES typically used to evaluate the health of a business are changing. Historical or, in the best case, short-term financial metrics, such as changes in sales and profits year after year, various expense ratios, and the balance sheet, do not provide a complete picture of a company's current and future performance. What's missing? Indicators of significant long-term growth potential, such as growth of customer bases, the ability to add-on sell, and access to customer information. These missing pieces are critical to customer equity and can greatly affect shareholder value.

America Online (AOL) is an example of a firm for which traditional measures provide an incomplete assessment of the firm's health. The current success of AOL shows that firms can create customer equity even while annual earnings lag. Table 8-1 shows a consolidated statement of AOL's earnings and operations from 1997 to 1999. From a customer equity perspective, it is interesting to note in table 8-1 that the majority of AOL's revenues come from subscription services. One can infer from this that the overall value of AOL is in part driven by the current and future value of its customer base. Table 8-2 shows the highs and lows of AOL's stock prices over the same period. The two tables together indicate that AOL's investments in customer equity development likely have played a role in the rapid appreciation of its stock.

**Table 8-1**

AOL's Earnings and Operations, 1997–1999

|  | Year Ended June 30 | | |
|  | 1999 | 1998 | 1997 |
|---|---|---|---|
| Subscription services revenues | $3,321 | $2,183 | $1,478 |
| Advertising, commerce, and other revenues | 1,000 | 543 | 308 |
| Enterprise solutions revenues | 456 | 365 | 411 |
| Total revenues | $4,777 | $3,091 | $2,197 |
| Operating income[a] | $ 578 | $ 66 | $ 6 |
| Net income[a] | $ 396 | $ 59 | $ 10 |
| EPS (in dollars)[a] | $ 0.34 | $ 0.06 | $ 0.01 |
| EBITDA[b] | $ 968 | $ 302 | $ 111 |
| AOL members (in thousands) | 17,619 | 12,535 | 8,636 |
| Employees (in whole numbers) | 12,100 | 8,500 | 7,400 |

[a]On a fully taxed basis before one-time charges.
[b]Earnings before interest, taxes, depreciation, amortization.

*Note:* Figures are in millions unless otherwise noted.

*Source:* America Online Annual Report, 1999. Available at http://corp.aol.com/annual/highlights/highlights.html. Used with permission.


**Table 8-2**

AOL Stock Prices: Highs and Lows

| For the Quarter Ended: | High ($) | Low ($) |
|---|---|---|
| September 30, 1997 | 10.06 | 7.06 |
| December 31, 1997 | 11.41 | 8.00 |
| March 31, 1998 | 17.47 | 10.31 |
| June 30, 1998 | 27.41 | 17.31 |
| September 30, 1998 | 35.13 | 17.50 |
| December 31, 1998 | 80.00 | 20.66 |
| March 31, 1999 | 153.70 | 67.00 |
| June 30, 1999 | 175.00 | 89.50 |

*Source:* America Online Annual Report, 1999. Available at http://corp.aol.com/annual/information/information.html. Used with permission.

Shifting to a customer equity focus requires that firms develop new ways to evaluate their business. In the separate chapters on acquisition, retention, and add-on selling we introduced accounting measures. Although those metrics are great for analyzing strategies independently, firms need a framework for assessing their entire business. In this chapter we introduce that framework, which is composed of two critical elements: the customer equity balance sheet and the customer equity flow statement. A customer equity balance sheet is a summary statement that is instrumental in analyzing the current level of a firm's customer equity. The customer equity flow statement is more detailed and helps to identify the sources of gains and losses in the firm's customer equity. These statements are important because ultimately these gains or losses in customer assets will translate into gains or losses in shareholder value.

## Customer Equity Balance Sheet

Several critical elements distinguish a customer equity balance sheet from a typical balance sheet. The first is the distinction between new and existing customers in a customer equity balance sheet, a distinction that reveals the differences in profitability of customers at different stages of the customer life cycle. Another important feature captured in the customer equity balance sheet is future cash flows from customers. These cash flows are projected based on customer retention rates and future spending behavior.

Using these two features, the customer equity balance sheet lists four sources of value: new customers, current period; new customers, future periods; retained customers, current period; and retained customers, future periods.

- *New-customer current profits:* This measure calculates the acquisition profit or loss for the cohort of customers acquired in the current period. (A *cohort* is a group of customers acquired at the same point in time.) Generally this measure is negative and may be viewed as a liability. When negative, this measure represents the minimum level of profits that are necessary in the future in order for the new customers to have a positive lifetime value. If the new-customer future profits are not greater than this amount, the firm should reexamine its customer acquisition strategy and consider the implications of the acquisition strategy on its retention and add-on selling efforts.

- *New-customer future profits:* Future customer equity for new customers equals the sum of discounted future profits for all periods after the initial period. This metric is an important indicator of changes in the firm's future customer equity. A firm cannot sustain its customer equity without a sound acquisition effort. If the future profitability outlook of a firm's newly acquired customers is repeatedly poor, then the firm may be ineffective in its balance and management of the customer equity strategies. Firms should monitor changes in the magnitude of this measure. The larger the projection of this metric, the more aggressively the firm should pursue the acquisition of the cohort.

- *Profit from retained customers, current year:* This measure calculates the current year's profits for all retained customers in all cohorts. This measure is generally what is represented by traditional performance metrics.

  Using this measure to make inferences about the firm's performance can be tricky. A firm that has few core customers and more early repeaters could report a low value for this number because the customer base has not evolved to where attrition rates are more stable or where add-on buying is more prevalent.

  Firms that have a customer equity focus should not become overly content with high levels of profit from retained customers in the current year. It is an important contributor to customer equity but is only a piece of the total equity. How the firm manages the future of the retained customers will make the most significant impact on total customer equity.

- *Profit from retained customers in future years:* This measure calculates the discounted future profits represented by retained customers from all customer cohorts. This metric should generally constitute a significant portion of a firm's customer equity because it reflects the retention and add-on selling efforts that are directed to the majority of the firm's customers over several periods. Most customer-focused firms understand the importance of this measure. The potentially large magnitude of this metric is what drives firms to adopt loyalty programs and customer-recapture programs.

**Table 8-3**
Customer Equity Balance Sheet

| | |
|---|---|
| New customers, current year | $ (4,500,000) |
| New customers, future years | $ 9,935,469 |
| Retained customers, current year | $18,474,694 |
| Retained customers, future years | $56,217,778 |
| Total customer equity | $80,127,941 |

The sum of these four metrics is the customer equity for a firm's entire customer base. Table 8-3 provides an example of a customer equity balance sheet. Formulas for computing the metrics in this chapter can be found on the Web site www.customerequity.com.

Each individual measure provides insight into a particular aspect of the firm's current or potential future performance, but their greatest value is when they are analyzed together. Looking at a total customer equity measure at a given point in time will not necessarily reveal weaknesses in the firm's strategies. In addition, firms can temporarily mask inefficient or ineffective customer relationship management strategies by only reporting current-year measures or the total customer equity. As previously mentioned, analyzing the impact of losses in the current year from new customers can only be determined by looking at the future value of those customers. Similarly, the total customer equity measure will not reveal negative trends in the acquisition strategy if the retention or add-on selling strategy is sound. Many new-economy companies can attest to the fact that the reverse is also true. Specifically, an aggressive acquisition strategy that is successful can temporarily present the guise of high levels of customer equity when in reality the firm is failing at the other aspects of customer management.

To see how a firm can use a customer equity balance sheet to assess its strategy and performance, consider the case study of Bluefly.com. This case study shows that the customer equity balance sheet can be derived from general sales and margin information that can be obtained from two sources: sales and marketing. A sales database that tracks individual customer purchases provides relevant information regarding sales and new and repeat customer counts. Marketing records provide necessary information on margins, marketing expenditures, and the customer responses to those expenditures.

## Case Study: Application of a Customer Equity Balance Sheet

Bluefly.com, in business since September 1998, sells clothing from brand-name designers such as Calvin Klein and Ralph Lauren at 25 percent to 75 percent discounts. The retailer buys directly from manufacturers and consolidators, as well as from retailers clearing out end-of-season merchandise. In addition, Bluefly.com features MyCatalog, the company's proprietary database search technology that allows a user to create a personalized catalog that features only the brands, sizes, and styles in which the user is interested. By the end of 2000, Bluefly.com carried 9,000 items from about 300 designer labels.

### Customer Equity Economics

In 1999 and 2000 Bluefly.com achieved the financial performance shown in table 8-4. To use these results to calculate Bluefly.com's customer equity, we have to make an assumption about customer retention since retention rate data are not publicly available. At the end of the third quarter of 2000, the company reported that about 50 percent of dollar sales were made to repeat customers. Given that retained customers tend to make more purchases, we can assume that their retention rate is at least 50 percent. Based on that, we conservatively assume a retention rate of 60 percent. (This estimate seems reasonable, though

**Table 8-4**
Bluefly.com's Financial Performance, 1999–2000

|  | 1999 | 2000 (E) |
|---|---|---|
| Revenue | $4,951,000 | $25,000,000 |
| Gross margins | 24% | 18.5% |
| Total number of customers | 25,000 | 150,000 |
| Number of customers acquired | 20,000 | 135,000 |
| Number of customers retained | 5,000 | 15,000 |
| Average order size per new customer | $85 | $90 |
| Average order size per repeat customer | $125 | $115 |
| Acquisition cost per customer | $180 | $60 |
| Retention cost per customer | $146 | $20 |

*Source:* Annual reports, press releases, and company Web site (http://www.bluefly.com).

**Table 8-5**

Bluefly.com's Customer Retention Tracking

|  | *1999* | *2000* | *2001* | *2002* | *2003* | *2004* |
|---|---|---|---|---|---|---|
| 1998 cohort | 5,000 | 3,000 | 1,800 | 1,080 | 648 | 389 |
| 1999 cohort | 20,000 | 12,000 | 12,000 | 12,000 | 12,000 | 12,000 |
| 2000 cohort |  | 135,000 | 81,000 | 48,600 | 29,160 | 17,496 |

*Note:* Assumed retention rate = 0.6.
*Source:* Estimates based on data from company reports.

we can run a sensitivity analysis to see how various levels of retention would affect customer equity.) Using this figure as Bluefly.com's customer retention rate, table 8-5 projects the number of customers that remain from each cohort in each year.

Based on these results and assumptions, we can construct the customer equity of Bluefly.com for 1999 and 2000. These balance sheets are shown in tables 8-6 and 8-7. In 1999, under these assumptions, Bluefly.com had a negative customer equity value of approximately $3.1 million, which was the result of relatively high retention and acquisition costs and a small customer base. By reducing retention and acquisition costs by more than 50 percent per customer and increasing the customer base dramatically, Bluefly.com was able to realize an increase in the value of their customer equity in 2000 to negative $2.5 million. (Bluefly.com's market capitalization was approximately $8 million in the fourth quarter of 2000.)

Although total customer equity increased substantially in absolute terms from 1999 to 2000, the improvement still left Bluefly.com with

**Table 8-6**

Bluefly.com's Customer Equity Balance Sheet, 1999

| | |
|---|---|
| New customers, current profits | $(3,192,000) |
| New customers, future profits | $ 602,115 |
| Retained customers, current profits | $ (580,000) |
| Retained customers, future profits | $ 88,760 |
| Total customer equity | $(3,081,125) |

*Note:* These projections are based on a 60% retention rate per period and a 15% discount rate, and are projected out for four years.
*Source:* Estimates based on data from company reports.

**Table 8-7**
Bluefly.com's Customer Equity Balance Sheet, 2000

| | |
|---|---|
| New customers, current profits | $(5,852,250) |
| New customers, future profits | $ 2,396,526 |
| Retained customers, current profits | $   263,625 |
| Retained customers, future profits | $   655,371 |
| Total customer equity | $(2,536,728) |

*Note:* These projections are based on a 60 percent retention rate per period and a
15 percent discount rate, and are projected out for four years.
*Source:* Estimates based on data from company reports.

negative customer equity. There are several reasons for this result. The first is the larger number of new customers generating negative margins in the current period, which is not completely subsidized by the number of retained customers. Another factor causing this negative equity is the smaller gross margins in 2000 that our calculations assumed to be fixed over time. The cost to acquire a new customer in 2000, though only one-third of what it was the previous year, was still $60. In addition, we estimate that the cost to retain or service a customer is approximately $20 per year (one-half of the selling, marketing, and fulfillment expenses after the acquisition portion has been subtracted). Because the average margin on a sale is approximately $20, it takes four transactions per customer in the first year just to make back the initial acquisition investment. In later years, the company only makes money in the second and ensuing sales each year to each customer.

In short, (again, based on the assumptions used in the model) Bluefly.com must dramatically improve its results by doing one or more of the following in order to build substantial customer equity:

- Lower acquisition costs (as has been done between 1999 and 2000), retention costs, or both

- Increase the retention rate

- Increase average ticket size

Lowering costs will improve Bluefly.com's customer equity, particularly in the short term. However, in the long term they also need to develop a sizeable core group of customers who can generate sufficient revenues through add-on selling or increased purchase value. This core group will compensate for the potential losses of newly acquired customers. This will take time but is definitely feasible.

## Customer Equity Flow Statement

The customer equity flow statement adds to the insights that can be derived from the customer equity balance sheet. Specifically, a customer equity flow statement is a summary statement compiled annually or at any selected time interval that indicates *changes* in customer equity. In addition to showing whether a firm's overall customer equity is increasing or decreasing, a flow statement shows the sources of the gains or losses. Table 8-8 provides an example.

The customer equity flow statement shows gains (or losses) in six categories: new customers, current and future periods; retained customers, current and future periods; and nonretained customers (defectors), current and future periods. (The defectors, of course, only show losses.) It is important to include defectors in a customer equity flow statement because they represent lost opportunity for the firm. Assuming that defectors would generate positive equity if they were retained, ignoring them will paint a more optimistic picture of a firm's performance than is warranted.

Because a customer equity flow statement reflects changes in customer equity, two essential types of data go into the computation of these metrics: retention rate dynamics and buying behavior patterns (e.g., increased purchase frequency, volume, or add-on buying). Changes in the retention rate are used to project the number of customers each period, and buying behavior patterns are used to derive per-customer margins each period. Period-by-period changes in these

**Table 8-8**
Customer Equity Flow Statement, 1999

| | |
|---|---|
| New customers, current period | $(4,500,000) |
| New customers, future periods | $ 9,935,469 |
| Retained customers, current period | $ 3,087,938 |
| Retained customers, future periods | $ 3,266,225 |
| Nonretained customers, current period | $(6,973,369) |
| Nonretained customers, future periods | $(6,547,402) |
| Net gains (losses) in customer equity | $(1,731,140) |

statistics (i.e., the number of new, retained, and lost customers and shifts in per-customer margin) are what drive the figures reported in the customer equity flow statement.

- *Gains (losses) from new customers, current and future periods:* Because these are new customers, there is no history from which to derive incremental changes in profits. Therefore, this measure is the same as the profits or losses for new customers that are reported on the customer equity balance sheet.

- *Gains (losses) from retained customers, current period:* This metric shows the incremental profits (or losses) in the current period that the firm gained by keeping a portion of the prior period's customers in the current period. Because add-on buying is more likely to occur during the retention phase of the relationship, accurate data on the margin associated with those purchases are critical to the computation of this metric.

- *Expected gains (losses) from retained customers, future periods:* Like the previous measure, this metric is valuable for demonstrating the incremental payout of retaining customers from one period to the next. However, this metric projects the payout into the future. To estimate this measure, firms must be able to forecast retention rates and the future spending behavior of their customers. This can be challenging without historical data that reflect these trends. Ideally this measure should never be negative. However, if a firm fails to carefully monitor customer behavior and implement de-marketing tactics when necessary, this measure could in fact be small or, in the extreme case, could be negative.

- *Expected lost profit from defecting customers, current period:* This metric focuses on the number of lost customers rather than retained customers. With this number and with projections about customer buying behavior, firms can compute the amount of value lost due to customer defections. Without this knowledge firms cannot truly know the effectiveness of their customer management efforts or adjust their marketing strategy appropriately.

- *Expected lost customer equity from defecting customers, future periods:* This final computation determines the loss in future equity represented by customers lost in the current period. This number should not always be viewed as a blemish on the firm's performance. Remember that the maximum retention potential for a firm is usually not 100 percent. Therefore, firms can use this measure as an indicator that their efforts and trade-offs are in the right direction when this number is low and fairly static. However, high values of this measure can suggest that a firm should implement a customer-recapture strategy, and dramatic shifts in this figure may indicate a lack of consistency in the firm's strategic balance.

It can be difficult to foresee a company's future growth or lack of growth. Viewing the flow statement in its entirety can help management and analysts to diagnose whether the increased sales and profitability in the current period are occurring at the expense of long-term customer equity. Similarly, the statement can indicate whether management is increasing long-term shareholder value through greater value associated with the firm's marketing system. How? If gains from new customers do not exceed losses associated with customer defections, the firm is not increasing its economic value. The implication, then, is that the firm's marketing system is inefficient: Shareholder wealth is not improved. For shareholders, therefore, a customer equity flow statement can be vital to forecasting the future value of their investment.

## Summary

Managing customer equity is a challenging task. It is more challenging if firms do not have appropriate metrics and frameworks that can assess their efforts. Individual metrics for acquisition, retention, and add-on selling are only the beginning. Firms that wish to manage customer equity over the long term must develop a customer equity balance sheet that distinguishes between new and retained customers and between current and future profits. Additionally, to dynamically adjust their balance of strategies and provide value to their shareholders, firms need to continuously analyze flows in customer value through a customer equity flow statement that accounts for new, retained, and lost customer value.

# 9

## ORGANIZING FOR CUSTOMER EQUITY

A CLEVER OBSERVER once noted that, by definition, every organization is perfectly structured to achieve exactly what it does. The fact that very few companies today maximize the value of their customer assets suggests that most will need to change their organizations in order to adopt a customer equity model successfully. This chapter focuses on customer equity's organizational requirements and the mechanisms a firm can use to achieve them.

### Principles of Organizational Design

Managers have a much broader range of leverage points for organizing at their disposal than the typical reliance on structural box-and-wire charts suggests. As figure 9-1 shows, companies can draw on five organizing weapons: structure, management systems and processes, skills, beliefs, and leadership behaviors.[1]

Change usually starts with organizational structure. By selecting the appropriate dominant dimension around which to organize (e.g., customer segment, functional activity, geography), clearly setting the roles and authorities of each part of the organization, and defining the points of interaction among units, companies can significantly accelerate progress toward their goals.

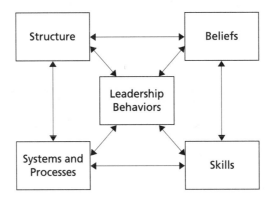

**Figure 9-1** Basic Organizing Model

Management systems and processes—the ways in which activities are coordinated and in which information flows from group to group and from individual to individual—are the next piece of the puzzle. These include a wide range of mechanisms, from measurement and reward systems to database management.

People and their skill sets bring structures and processes to life. Selecting, acquiring, and deploying the array of talents required to make a system work presents the next critical organizing challenge. The types of people and skill sets needed vary dramatically from business to business, particularly at the customer interface level. If executing the selected customer equity strategy calls for skill sets significantly different from those currently at work in a company, the challenge and potential displacement associated with retraining, adding, and terminating members of the organization can create formidable barriers to successful organization for driving customer equity.

A company's belief system, or culture, binds its people, processes, and structure together. This includes both the guiding beliefs of the company and the daily beliefs of the people who inhabit it. The Johnson & Johnson Credo offers a prototypical example of an effective statement of guiding beliefs, which during the Tylenol scare translated directly into action. Daily beliefs typically are expressed in terms of "how things really get done around here," that is, what can get people in trouble, get them ahead, and so on.

Leadership behavior, in turn, provides crucial support to the belief system. The actions of the firm's senior members set the tone of the organization and establish its priority activities. If the top management is out there greeting customers, chances are that others will get the hint. Employees are amazingly adept at differentiating between what managers profess to want and what their actions suggest that they really want, and they tend to emulate the latter.[2] Leadership behaviors that are inconsistent with desired direction rapidly will undermine any progress made using the four other organizing elements.

These five organizing elements do not stand alone, but need to work in concert. Success lies in achieving a coherent mix and in keeping that mix responsive to the company's needs. In many cases, one element can be substituted for another. For example, in most consumer-products organizations, rapid rotation of people through brand management positions (and across brands and categories) not only is accepted as a fact of life but also is seen as an appealing job feature. As a result, an "oral history" of what works and what doesn't, found in many other types of organizations, often does not exist in packaged-goods companies. ("I don't know what they were doing here in Fluffy Flakes last year. I was the brand assistant over in Franks 'n Wieners at the time.") Lengthening tenures and slowing job rotation might solve this problem, but only at the substantial risk of losing key employees who view mobility as part of the social contract. As an alternative, managers could accept that dependence on individuals' knowledge will not work at such companies; by installing the appropriate information repositories and knowledge-management systems, they can substitute institutional knowledge for individual memory. In the terms of figure 9-1, this amounts to substituting management systems for people skills. It is also important to know which tools best suit a given set of circumstances. For example, in some organizations, using compensation to spur customer acquisition (e.g., paying sales representatives for new customers) may work more effectively than using leadership behaviors or structural change (e.g., naming a vice president of customer acquisition).

A final note: Although this chapter describes some ideal organization types, there is no such thing as a perfect organization in the real world. As a result, the organizing thoughts presented here should be regarded as a set of starting points, not as final prescriptions.

## Organizational Imperatives

Organizational imperatives are the functional outputs that a company must achieve in order to succeed. As such, it is usually possible to identify the implicit organizational imperatives of a company by inspecting how it is organized and by asking what goals would have shaped such an approach. For example, consider 3M, with its structure of dozens of semiautonomous divisions, largely independent management systems within divisions, explicit goals for the percentage of revenues that must be derived from new products, and widely publicized stories about the inventors of successful new offerings. These suggest that 3M has organized to achieve a set of imperatives focused on inventing, commercializing, and exploiting technologies, in support of an overall corporate direction of innovation. This comes at some cost, of course. No matter how hard it tries, 3M probably will never reach the streamlined efficiency of rivals who imitate rather than innovate as a way of life. Nor will it have as tight a focus on customer equity as a company with similar product breadth that is organized around industry verticals or major accounts.

Many types of professional-services firms build themselves around three imperatives: the ability to sustain long-term, multi-engagement relationships with client companies; the apprenticeship of junior staff to take on increasingly multifaceted roles as senior members of the firm; and the leverage of the same junior staff to maximize revenues and profits per partner. These types of companies emphasize customer retention, as indicated by the fact that "relationship officers" are typically among the firm's most senior members.

By contrast, many computer services and outsourcing companies, such as EDS, focus on signing long-term deals with customers and then on minimizing delivery costs on contracted services to maximize profit extraction. From the perspective of customer equity, these companies are strongly acquisition oriented. As time passes, it will be interesting to see how the natural conflicts between the customer-acquisition imperatives of computer services firms such as EDS, CSC, and Cap Gemini and the relationship orientations of their acquired consulting firms (A.T. Kearney, Index, Gemini Consulting, Ernst & Young) play out.

Companies that plan to take a customer equity approach to their markets must achieve the eight organizational imperatives listed in box 9-1. First of all, they must know their customers, both in the aggregate and at the individual level. An important element of this knowledge is the ability to measure customer equity per individual. They also must be able to manage customer acquisition, retention, and add-on selling, both as individual capabilities and as an optimized set. To do this, they

---

**Box 9-1**  Organizational Imperatives for Customer
Equity Management

1. Know your customers.

2. Measure the asset value of each customer.

3. Manage acquisition.

4. Manage retention.

5. Manage add-on selling.

6. Balance acquisition, retention, and add-on selling.

7. Manage customer portfolios.

8. Tailor the marketing mix.

---

must develop the ability to understand and manage portfolios of prospects and customers who are at various stages in the customer life cycle and who have markedly different responses to acquisition, retention, and add-on selling expenditures. Finally, the most successful customer equity organizations will be able to tailor all the elements of the marketing mix at the level of the individual customer.

## Structure

A firm's structure must support its most critical organizational imperatives. With a customer equity approach, a number of structural designs may apply. For instance, if a firm's customer population is fairly homogeneous in its wants, needs, and buying behaviors, but heterogeneous in its response to acquisition, retention, and add-on selling programs, it may make sense to structure its marketing organization around acquisition, retention, and add-on selling functions. If longitudinal management of customers throughout their life cycles is the most critical imperative, the creation of cross-functional teams that take responsibility for individual customers or customer cohorts may work better.

Let's take a closer look at these two structural alternatives. Figure 9-2 shows a sample organizational chart for the former. In this somewhat simplified model for a consumer-services company, three positions report directly to the senior marketing executive: the director of

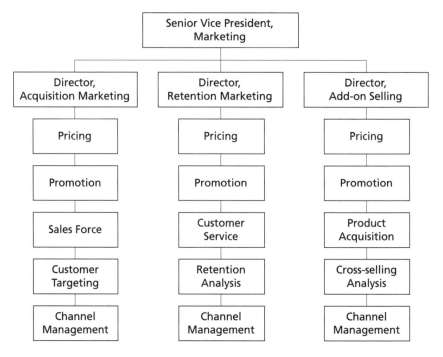

**Figure 9-2**    Organizational Chart Structured around the Major Elements of
                  Customer Equity Creation

acquisition marketing, the director of retention marketing, and the
director of add-on selling. Each of these three, in turn, has responsibility for those elements of pricing, promotion, and channel management
that serve his or her mission. For example, the director of acquisition
marketing has responsibility for the pricing of items used primarily to
attract new customers, and the director of retention marketing takes
responsibility for promotions designed to reactivate dormant customer
relationships.

   In addition, each director has responsibility for specific subfunc-
tions. In the figure 9-2 model, the acquisition director supervises a sales
force primarily geared toward customer acquisition and is responsible
for prospect targeting, which includes the design of product and service offerings specifically aimed at prospects.

   The retention director oversees retention analysis and customer
service. This part of the organization customizes the various elements
of the marketing mix according to the priorities of customer retention.
Some firms have created separate departments that focus exclusively on

customer loyalty or retention. MBNA America, for example, has instituted a "SWAT" team that actively pursues customers who cancel their
credit cards. Because of the efforts of this team, MBNA successfully
retains about half of the customers who attempt to defect.[3] Gillette
North America has a vice president of business relations who has as one
of his major responsibilities the task of cultivating relationships with
major retailers and distributors.[4]

The add-on selling director, in addition to handling pricing, promotion, and channel responsibilities, conducts analyses that identify
cross-selling tactics and products for cross-selling according to their
potential to increase customer equity.

The strength of this structure is that it directs attention to each of
the three major elements of customer equity creation, and by doing so
breaks with traditional organizing structures based on product groupings. It also reframes, in a very clear way, the role of product portfolio
management as the establishment of a portfolio of products and services that can be cross-sold to create customer equity.

At the same time, because of its single-minded focus on the organizational imperative of managing acquisition, retention, and add-on
selling as individual capabilities, this particular structure is less effective
at achieving other imperatives. For example, balancing resources across
the three directors' groups and mediating disputes among them (such
as whether the acquisition director's introductory promotions damage
the retention function's ability to extract full prices later on) will
require either intervention by senior marketing management or the
establishment of set management processes that link the three marketing subdivisions. Furthermore, it is quite possible that by focusing so
heavily on knowing the customer in three different ways, this organization will fail to understand the "whole" customer throughout his or
her life cycle. As suggested earlier, these limitations make this structure
best suited to situations in which the distinctions among the three customer equity elements are much greater than the differences among
individual customers. Or, in the language of the imperatives of box
9-1, this structure best suits situations in which the critical imperatives
of managing acquisition, retention, and add-on selling take precedence
over those of deep customer knowledge, customer portfolio management, and balance among approaches.

The second structural model, that of cross-functional teams,
applies to the opposite situation, in which success hinges on detailed

customer knowledge and precise tailoring of the marketing mix. In this model, customer development management teams (CDMTs) are the key structural element. Every CDMT specializes in a particular customer or customer segment. These teams manage all of the activities (e.g., sales, marketing, service, and distribution) that involve their respective customers. Customers with very similar needs, preferences, and behaviors can be classified as a segment and managed by one CDMT. This prevents duplicated efforts and promotes economies of scale.

A typical CDMT includes a representative from marketing, customer service, accounting, and R&D or product development. Each representative becomes an expert on the CDMT's assigned customer or segment and applies this knowledge to his or her operations. The marketing representative takes responsibility for all marketing to the customer or customer group, the accounting representative manages and monitors the customer's or group's financial status, the R&D representative finds technical or product solutions to meet the customer's or group's particular needs, and so on.

This structural approach enables the company to appear to the customer as a unified entity rather than as collection of independent units with varying levels of responsibility and accountability. Consider the counterexample of a pharmaceuticals firm that was structured around its brands. The firm had multiple sales forces, each of which sold different products to the same client base. Physicians often became annoyed when one sales representative could not answer questions about or provide samples of a product sold by another representative. After years of operating this way, the organization restructured to eliminate this major problem.

Of course, the integrative nature of the cross-functional structure and its focus on the customer as its dominant dimension also present problems. Unless a company takes care, CDMTs have a tendency to fragment functional resources, especially in R&D and channel management. Also, having a single group in charge of acquisition, retention, and add-on selling to a group of customers naturally weakens the focus on each of the three elements individually.

How does a firm decide which of these—or other structures—best fits its needs? It does so based on its organizational imperatives and their relative importance. By assessing the importance of each imperative to its business, a firm can select the appropriate dominant structural dimension for its marketing activities. After that, it can begin to build the necessary linkages to other organizational units.

## *Functional Roles*

Regardless of the structure a firm chooses for its marketing activities, the adoption of a customer equity approach requires significant changes in the roles of several other functions. Information Technology, for example, focuses its activities on creating database analysis systems that provide information on customer needs and on customer responsiveness to marketing actions. Marketing Services—or a new "liaison" organization—takes on the role of translating customer data into insights that marketing managers can use. Whether Marketing formally reorganizes around acquisition, retention, and add-on selling or not, accountability needs to be assigned to ensure that marketing programs directly address these strategies. Market Research, which in many organizations now focuses on customer characterization and market-size analysis, must be reoriented toward the measurement and management of customer affinity. Outside agency relationships, traditionally organized around marketing-mix elements such as advertising and promotion execution, need to be reframed to highlight the role that each agency relationship plays in retention or acquisition. Accounting must take charge of analyzing and providing reports on customer equity, and must make the link between customer equity and growth in shareholder value. Finally, Product Development, which today is generally technology or product based, must rethink its portfolio of products and services in terms of both acquisition offerings and the relevant assorted offerings that can be add-on sold to the firm's customer base.

In addition, brands play a different role in customer equity–oriented companies than they do in traditional marketing schemes. The emphasis shifts from building brand equity as an end in itself to building brands that strengthen the affinity between customer and provider. Consider here the emergence of Internet brands. Despite dire predictions that the emergence of the Internet would result in the death of brands, new brands such as Amazon.com now represent signposts of assurance in the shifting world of the Web. In many cases, they have done so by moving beyond credibility (keeping promises) to anticipation (getting ahead of customer needs), honesty (putting customer interests first), and a one-to-one relationship (knowing the customer). By providing these affinity-oriented benefits, these providers have built highly loyal customer bases that can be mined for customer equity. In the process, they have built powerful brands. The value of the customer franchise—not the value of the brand per se—has been their driving force.

In other words, customer equity management demands an organizational structure built around the creation of, and capitalization on, customer affinity. This structure must focus, across functions, on the imperatives of knowing customers and their value and of managing acquisition, retention, and add-on selling in an integrated way. Once in place, these structural elements will receive the reinforcement they need from the appropriate management processes and systems.

## Systems and Processes

The organizing imperatives provided in box 9-1 offer a firm its best guide for designing management systems and processes that maximize customer equity.

### Information Systems

The first imperative, knowing your customers by understanding their behavior, indicates the need for advanced database management. A firm must have the ability to develop sophisticated customer databases and to analyze them for information on customer needs and on customer responsiveness to specific marketing actions. The insights derived from such analyses facilitate effective communications with current customers as well as efficient customer acquisition efforts.

### Accounting Systems

A customer equity organization depends on its accounting systems for the measurement of customer equity. These systems evaluate the effectiveness of acquisition, retention, and add-on selling investments, analyze the payback from each investment, and determine the optimal allocation of resources among acquisition, retention, and add-on selling. This accounting, in aggregate, also provides a foundation for linking customer equity directly to shareholder value creation.

The development of full-blown information systems that can calculate the asset value of each individual customer presents a daunting task, but a firm does not have to start with such a complex approach. Many of the analyses needed to estimate the costs and rewards of acquisition, retention, and add-on selling can be done on the back of a cocktail napkin, at least at the aggregate level. In other words, systems for understanding customer equity need not be huge enterprise-wide models from the outset. A firm can institute simple processes at first, while management reviews its options regarding more powerful systems capable of dynamic analyses of individual customer value.

## *Performance and Rewards*

Performance measurement and reward systems are central to the successful operation of a customer equity organization. All too often employees—especially those in the lower ranks—view their relationships with the organization as somewhat adversarial or irrelevant to their personal goals. Take the case of a salesperson who has the choice of calling on two clients. One client has been a customer for several years but is hard to contact, unreceptive to salespeople, and very difficult to call on. It takes several sales calls to close one sale. Still, this client has the potential to buy significant amounts of products and services on an ongoing basis, and therefore represents high potential customer equity. The second client is brand new and represents about half the amount of business—and half the customer equity—that the first client does. This client, however, is friendlier, more accessible, and much easier to call on, and appears eager to make an immediate small purchase. Which client is the salesperson more likely to call on? Probably the new one, because of the lower level of effort required and the more easily visible near-term sales potential. The sales manager, in contrast, would probably advise the salesperson to call on the old client, who has the greater profit potential, while also trying to acquire the new one. How does this sales manager motivate the sales representative to call on both?

The answer to this lies in the firm's employee incentive program and its means of employee evaluation. In order to motivate employees to retain profitable customers and to build the existing business, management must evaluate them on how well they manage their customers and prospects. One way to do this is to evaluate sales employees on their customer acquisition and retention rates in addition to using more traditional sales measures. Similarly, customer service employees should be evaluated not just on the number of calls that they handle, but also on the rate at which they successfully resolve a customer's concerns and retain the customer. It is important that the measurement and rewarding of behaviors that build customer equity not be limited to members of the marketing staff. Instead, members of all functions whose activities affect customer acquisition, retention, and add-on selling (including, for instance, members of channel management groups and those responsible for developing product and service portfolios) should be measured and rewarded for work that builds customer equity.

### Support Systems

Of course, employees who are measured and rewarded for customer equity creation need supporting tools. In the early 1990s, British Airways realized that it needed to revamp its approach to customer relations. Traditionally this department played a defensive role; its job was to insulate the organization from unhappy customers. Customer relation employees investigated consumer complaints and then assigned blame for those complaints to other areas. This created an adversarial relationship between the customer relations department and other functional areas. The fact that customer relation employees were evaluated on their backlog of work but not on the quality of their customer service aggravated the situation. In this environment it took an average of more than twelve weeks for the department to respond to customer correspondence, and the cost of compensating customers was rising rapidly.[5]

As a first step in its reengineering effort, British Airways established a process in which customer relation employees apologized for—and took ownership of—the problems referred to them by customers. To support this process, British Airways installed a computer system known as CARESS (Customer Analysis and Retention System). This system profiled each customer's case history and could be accessed by employees across all functional areas. As an employee interacted with or performed activities that affected the customer, he or she could update the customer profile. Thus the customer's needs could be understood and satisfied more efficiently.

Like British Airways, Fidelity Investments's Institutional Group discovered that it needed a system containing detailed customer profiles that multiple employees could use easily. At the time, Fidelity had a three-day turnaround time for resolving customer complaints. This long response time, which increased customer frustration, stemmed partly from the fact that when a customer's Fidelity contact person was unavailable, the call was forwarded to a common pool and was answered by a person with no knowledge of the customer. To rectify this problem, Fidelity established a new system: If a client could not reach the usual Fidelity contact, the call would be forwarded to a backup person who had full access to the client's profile at the touch of a button.[6]

The creation of a customer profile database that is updated and accessible across functional areas institutionalizes the input of customer information that can be disseminated throughout the organization. (This database should serve as an operational database. A separate database, drawn from this one, can be used for analytical purposes.) The customer profile database also serves another important need. As demonstrated in the British Airways and Fidelity examples, it can act as an important communication tool across or within a firm's functional units. As each functional area learns more about the customer, the entire company can learn more about the customer.

What should a customer profile contain? In addition to basic demographic information, a customer profile ideally should contain information on the customer's purchase history, payment history, product or service complaint history, and marketing history (i.e., what marketing tactics the firm has directed at the customer). A complete profile also should contain an estimate of the customer's asset value and an estimated percentile of where that value ranks with regard to the customer equity of the firm's other customers. At a glance, any employee should be able to recognize a customer's value and serve that customer appropriately. In some instances this may entail making special concessions to highly valued customers.

To summarize, customer equity management requires systems and processes that further the understanding of customer behaviors, identify customer asset values, measure and reward employees for actions that build customer equity, and support employees in their efforts to take appropriate actions in serving customers. Systems and processes also serve to counteract the inherent limitations of a company's chosen organizational structure. For example, in a structure divided into acquisition, retention, and add-on selling units, processes and systems are needed that link the three together across the organization. This will help compensate for the structure's weaknesses in managing the same customers over time. A CDMT organization, on the other hand, needs metrics that evaluate returns on acquisition, retention, and add-on selling across customer groups, and that track acquisition to ensure an adequate influx of new members into the customer portfolio.

## People and Skills

At the organizational level, a firm's required skills follow from the imperatives outlined in box 9-1. At subgroup and individual levels, however, necessary skills fall into five categories:

- Technical

- Analytical

- Synthesis

- Design

- Communication and interaction

Technical skills include the database management and customer behavior calculation capabilities noted earlier in this chapter. Particularly critical is the ability to integrate information across multiple databases, because most organizations today store relevant customer behavioral data in several, often incompatible, databases. Finance and accounting skills that enable thinking in customer equity terms also are very important.

Analytical skills include the ability to translate customer behavioral data into guidance for specific marketing activities, to evaluate the effectiveness of (and returns on) acquisition and retention investments, and to decipher customer responses to—and the customer equity resulting from—specific marketing initiatives. This kind of skill set likely will require either a new breed of individual who bridges the worlds of management information, marketing, and finance or a close alliance among members of those functions, along with a strong set of supporting analytical systems. For example, individuals and teams charged with acquiring new customers need extensive knowledge of the existing customer base, as well as the ability to apply that knowledge to the assessment of noncustomers' likely responsiveness to marketing and their overall value potential. They need to understand the profile of existing, profitable customers and be able to identify the characteristics of these customers in prospects. This makes data mining skills essential, in order to build and run models on customers' price elasticities and to devise prospect-rating frameworks.

Although analytic skill—the ability to drill down for understanding—is crucial, it is just as important that customer equity organizations have the ability to step back, see the bigger picture, and integrate their actions across customers, products, and organizations. Customer equity management succeeds by creating a cooperative whole from a company's diverse parts, which otherwise have a tendency to develop conflicting interests and goals. Synthesis skills support this effort, whether the challenge at hand is to derive customer behavior drivers from seas of data or, at a higher level, to manage portfolios of customers and product offerings simultaneously. Companies need the ability to take a portfolio view and to understand individual customers, products, and services in the larger context of customer equity. Unfortunately, synthesis skills are often in short supply, particularly in engineering- and finance-based organizations.

Once technical and analytical skills have provided the inputs, and synthesis skills have recognized the patterns, design skills are necessary to tailor the marketing mix to individual customers or customer cohorts. In a customer equity organization, slavish adherence to standard formats does not lead to success. Instead, managers need to think on their feet to match pricing, promotion, channel, communication, and product policies and programs to the needs of individual customers or customer subsegments, paying constant attention to how the costs of these tailored programs relate to potential returns.

Finally, customer equity management draws on a new set of communication and interaction skills. This skill set includes interpersonal skills used in services and industrial marketing settings to acquire and retain customers, and customer service skills that support retention and add-on selling. It also includes the communication skills needed to tailor multiple marketing messages to diverse subsegments and to develop strong brand personalities that both speak to the customers a company wishes to acquire and provide a broad enough umbrella to enable effective add-on selling to existing customers.

## Beliefs

As mentioned earlier, it is virtually impossible to make the change from traditional market management to customer equity management if the interests of employees are not aligned with those of the company. If employees do not believe that developing and capturing customer equity is in their own interests, it is highly likely that old patterns of behavior will persist and that despite any structural reorganization or changes in management systems, customer equity will not be captured.

Happily, companies have several levers to use in changing an organization's belief system. First of all, it is important to make the value of the customer a highly visible goal. British Airways made it clear that customer satisfaction had top priority when it launched a formal effort to "champion the customer," invested in increased gathering of customer feedback, and positioned itself publicly as "The World's Favourite Airline." The customer equity–oriented organization needs to go beyond this and make not only customer satisfaction but also customer asset value a highly visible goal. It can do this by emphasizing the roles of acquisition, retention, and add-on selling in building customer equity and by setting explicit goals for customer equity attainment. In addition, employees must know and understand the importance of customer management to the firm, the importance of customer management to themselves, and their impact on the customer–firm relationship. Not an easy task! It is probably easiest to communicate to employees the importance of customer retention, for example, by highlighting simple statistics such as "a 5 percent increase in customer retention can increase firm profitability between 25 percent and 85 percent."[7] Although the detailed application of a customer equity approach enables a far more extensive understanding of customer value than these sorts of aggregate measures convey, rough and ready statistics do make the point with employees—generally far better than lengthy lectures on the intricacies of customer equity calculation can.

As highlighted earlier with the examples of CARESS at British Airways and the call rollover system at Fidelity, employees need support tools to succeed in their new roles. Alignment of measures and rewards (both of the financial and "attaboy" types) with the desired direction also serves as a powerful change mechanism for beliefs.

Employee empowerment is final step on this road of cultural change. Even if a firm's structure centers on the customer, the structure is worthless if the employees responsible for those customers cannot make decisions. All too often decision-making power resides with upper-level—or sometimes middle-level—managers who do not come into contact with customers.

In an alternative to this traditional chain of authority, upper-level managers establish general strategies and objectives, while individual customer-facing employees or CDMTs decide how to implement them for each customer or customer segment. This creates consistency across the organization in terms of its goals and objectives, yet allows each customer or segment to be handled individually and in the most appropriate manner. Benefits of this approach include shorter response times to customer issues, the heightened perception among customers that they are valued by the firm, and the placement of decision-making responsibility in the hands of those who know the customer best, resulting in more satisfying and appropriate customer–firm interactions. Perhaps most important, this approach encourages employee ownership of the customer–firm relationship, increasing the level of employee buy-in to the significance of customer management and customer equity maximization.

## Leadership Behaviors

The easiest way for senior managers to undermine change is with their actions. As noted earlier, employees may hear executives' words, but they watch their actions. The moment the espoused beliefs of the organization vary from the daily beliefs demonstrated by action, productive change grinds to a halt.

In a customer equity organization, everyone—from entry-level workers to the CEO—needs to adopt the objective of managing customers for value. The entire organization must recognize the customer as an asset to be cultivated. First American Bank Corporation, for example, found a direct relationship between the level of management commitment to high-quality service and its customers' perceptions of the bank's level of service. If employees viewed bank branch management as having a high level of commitment to service, then external customers tended to rate the bank's service highly. The reverse also was true.[8]

In other words, a customer equity approach requires careful planning not only of how a firm engages its front-line employees, but also of how it engages, motivates, and aligns the actions of its managers. This includes explicit identification of desired behaviors, open discussion with managers about expectations, and active correction of any behavior that undermines the realization of customer value.

## Imperatives for "Pure Type" Organizations

Some companies focus their efforts on only one of customer equity's core strategies (e.g., an acquisition-based firm). A look at the organizational imperatives that apply to these companies sheds light on the capabilities required to manage each of the three strategies within a balanced approach, as well as on the key organizational capabilities needed by companies that closely resemble these pure types.

For an acquisition-based company that seeks to maximize customer equity, one organizational imperative takes precedence: maximizing the value of customer relationships during acquisition, when that value is largely set. To do this, the organization's design must focus on targeting, reaching, and closing desirable prospects in a cost-effective way. Figure 9-3 shows that, in addition to basic customer equity competencies in database management and financial modeling, an acquisition-oriented organization needs two core capabilities: customer insight and brand management. Customer insight refers to developing an understanding of targeted customers, as in the case of modeling work done by credit card issuers. This insight guides product and service design and targeting efforts. Here, brand management means developing a brand positioning that appeals to prospects and then using various media to create awareness among targeted customers of the company's offerings and benefits.

For a retention-oriented company, the key imperative is maintaining and maximizing the value of customer relationships throughout their life cycles. To achieve this, the company must excel at mass-customized marketing—tailoring the marketing mix to microsegments or individual customers. Under this rubric fall one-to-one communication programs, loyalty and reactivation programs, customer-specific and segment-specific pricing and promotions, product and service offerings that make customers feel as if the company knows them personally, and personalized customer service. Whereas an acquisition-oriented company generally should have an organizational structure built around its prospecting function, a retention company should be organized around customers or customer cohorts, with strong management processes and systems that support tailoring of the marketing mix.

For the add-on selling company, the major imperative is developing a relevant set of offerings and bringing them to customers. As shown in figure 9-3, the add-on selling organization focuses on cross-selling expertise, effective communication of its offerings and their benefits to consumers, development of a coherent brand personality that can reach across multiple offerings, and careful management of the offering portfolio. The final item is the most important of these four supporting capabilities. Portfolio managers must prevent the offering

**Retention**
- Customized Marketing
  - Communication
  - Reactivation
  - Loyalty
  - Pricing/Promotions
  - Customer Service

**Acquisition**
- Customer Insight
  - Offer Design
  - Targeting
- Brand Management
  - Positioning
  - Awareness

**Add-on Selling**
- Cross-selling
- Customer Communication
- Brand Personality
- Product Portfolio Management

**Figure 9-3**  Capabilities of "Pure Type" Organizations

set from becoming too broad (alienating customers with irrelevant offers), unlinked (creating an offering set with a total value worth less than the sum of its parts), or too narrow (underleveraging the potential asset value of the customer). The add-on selling company has strong portfolio management and brand management groups, a powerful sales organization, and a marketing function that focuses on identification of potential areas for add-on selling as well as establishment and maintenance of the umbrella brand.

## Summary

By now, it should be apparent that organizing to capture customer equity means a great deal more than naming a director of customer relationship management, installing computer systems that can calculate customer equity, or making speeches about the importance of customers. Successful customer equity practitioners will identify and prioritize the organizing imperatives that apply to their specific situations and markets, and then use a coordinated mix of structure, systems, skills, beliefs, and behaviors to change organizational capabilities and achieve the desired imperatives. This organizing task is complex and likely will result in considerable discomfort for many traditionally organized companies. But the ability to pull it off will be a key feature distinguishing those companies that move forward to reap the benefits of asset-based customer management from those that do not.

# 10

## THE FUTURE OF
## CUSTOMER EQUITY

S o FAR, this book has identified how a firm can design customer
equity strategies in the current business environment. We now look
at trends that will almost certainly affect the future of customer equity,
and their implications. Specifically, we focus on technological trends,
the online economy, outsourcing and alliances, new valuation models,
branding, and the all-important issue of privacy.

Table 10-1 summarizes emerging trends in the marketplace and
their effects on customer equity and its component parts. Many of
these forces will help to remove existing barriers to effective customer
equity management. Others, such as increased privacy concerns among
the public, may strengthen these barriers or create new ones.

### Technological Trends

There are three relevant technological trends: increasing computing
power, broadening software availability, and increased scarcity of the
expertise needed to take advantage of either.

#### Computing Power

Moore's Law has not yet been repealed: Computing power continues
to double approximately every eighteen months. Importantly, this law

**Table 10-1**
Effects of Forces on Customer Equity

| Force | Overall Customer Equity | | Effects on | | |
|---|---|---|---|---|---|
| | *Positives* | *Threats* | *Acquisition* | *Retention* | *Add-on Selling* |
| Increased computing power and software availability | Increases affordability and ease of analysis | Same capabilities available to competitors | Improved ability to target attractive prospects selectively | Discerning needs/tailoring offerings easier | Easier to add integrative value to bundled offerings |
| Online/Internet economy | Many more sources of customer behavioral data | Potential foreclosure from data; customer power | Key awareness avenue | Freshness, links as keys to retention; lower switching barriers | Ability to form virtual bundled offerings |
| Smart products/interactions | Increased data flow on customer behavior | Data deluge | Easier targeting, if data can be obtained | Potential switching barrier | Improved tailoring of add-on offerings |
| Outsourcing | Allows focus on activities that build customer equity | Risks outsourcing activities critical to customer equity | Beware outsourcing of "core" customer equity levers | | |
| Alliance networks | Improved ability to match customer desires exactly | Potential loss of control or customer contact | Use customer access as key alliance criterion | Occupy nodal positions in data flows | Potential for benefits of tailoring without costs |
| Warfare for loyalty | Increases importance of customer equity approach | — | Attack "soft underbelly" of retention companies | Focus on high-equity customers | Apply strict relevance test to add-on offerings |

| | | | | | |
|---|---|---|---|---|---|
| Channel proliferation | Customer equity a key tool for prioritizing channels | Expensive; difficult to cover entire markets | Consider additional acquisition avenues; beware costs | May need broader channel array to retain customers | Think of "add-on" in channel terms |
| One-to-one marketing communications | Increases affordability and effectiveness | — | Practice razor-sharp acquisition targeting | Tailor one-to-one retention messages; beware acquisition "cherry-pickers" | Sharpen targeting of add-on messages to individual customers |
| Customer/consumer power | Increases necessity | Makes value extraction tougher | Claim only what you can deliver | Beware front-end overinvestment | Focus on value to customers of any add-ons |
| Disintermediation | Direct access to customers | Threats to "traditional" roles | Consider new avenues to reach prospects | Anticipate shifts in value network | Add integrative or information value |
| Privacy concerns | Give value, gain trust | Potential to get locked out | May need to pay for needed data | Value creators build switching barriers | Increased viability, reduced flexibility |

applies to data storage as well as to processing speed. Today, a high-powered personal computer is equivalent to a mainframe of fifteen years ago. Workstations have the power and storage space to maintain customer behavior databases for small- to medium-size companies. Currently—and certainly in the future—the hardware necessary to capture and process customer data is not an inhibitor of successful customer equity management.

At the same time, computer costs are dropping dramatically. This makes sophisticated data management affordable to smaller and smaller companies. With less costly storage hardware and the emergence of application service providers who sell storage services on an as-used basis, storage will be so plentiful and cheap that no firm will be able to use CPU or storage costs as an excuse to avoid creating and maintaining customer databases.

### Database Management Tools

The ability to manage customer databases efficiently using software tools continues to improve. The power and affordability of database management tools have increased exponentially, and they will continue to do so. (One authority on database marketing noted in 1999 that database prices had halved four times in six years.[1]) There are software programs available for as little as $6,000 that help companies to validate customer and prospect lists and to improve targeting.[2]

Improved database tools have substantial implications for the future of customer equity management. As the use of databases becomes simpler and more cost-effective, smaller and smaller companies will find it affordable to concentrate on customer equity as an objective and to use the approaches recommended in this book for acquisition, retention, and add-on selling.

In a variety of industries, increased use of databases will help change the rules of competition as companies convert traditional acquisition businesses into retention businesses. That is, decreasing data storage and manipulation costs will allow more and more businesses—such as those that were forced into a transaction business model by the sheer costs of understanding customers—to make the shift to add-on selling and relationship approaches.

### Staff Expertise

The main inhibitor to database marketing and customer equity is staff expertise. Just when technology is making it possible for firms to manage larger and larger databases, the skilled people required to implement and manage these databases are becoming less and less available. Supply has not caught up with demand.

The first skill shortage is in statistics. Statisticians who can interpret and utilize customer databases are in great demand. However, very few schools train applied statisticians who can work with data to develop the types of models and analytical tools that customer equity businesses need. Statistics is not a glamorous field to business executives, and the path from statistics to general management is limited. (After all, one description of a statistician is a dull accountant.) This lack of a career path limits supply and will be a major constraint on the next generation of firms that want to implement customer equity management. Expert software and analytical packages for data mining will be needed to overcome the limited supply of statisticians.

The field of marketing also lacks adequate expertise. Most traditional marketing staffs have learned brand management but not customer management, and marketers often have limited quantitative skills. Customer equity marketing depends on the rigorous analysis of data, both customer and marketing, to design programs.

On the other hand, highly quantitative marketing specialists often do not have the creative skills needed to develop effective marketing programs. Identifying a firm's marketing problem, such as the lack of cost-effective customer acquisition, does not equal finding a solution. Customer equity management will require combining analytical and creative marketing skills.

The solution is not simple. First, customer equity management will require a new career path for technically sophisticated statisticians, who may lack management skills but who are essential to the organization's success. It will also require finding "ambidextrous" minds that draw on both left and right brains, marrying creative and quantitative marketing skills. Unfortunately, this is a bit like finding an artist who majored in mathematics. As an alternative, it may be possible to create teams that combine the quantitative and creative. Silicon Valley and its international counterparts have been able to develop this unique set of people, who are technically enabled and creative enough to develop new approaches to complex customer needs.

## The Online Economy

Clearly, e-commerce will have a tremendous impact on the strategy, tactics, and management of customer equity. We are not among those predicting that in the future all purchasing will take place online. Nonetheless, the sweep of electronic commerce has profound implications for customer equity, primarily because of the availability of better information.

The online economy raises several questions that affect customer equity:

- How will the ease of switching intensify competition, and will it mean that retention marketing will no longer be at the forefront of customer marketing?

- Can firms erect barriers to exit that combat the ease of switching online?

- Will brands or channels own the customer?

### The Switching Dilemma

There is an old adage in retailing: Location, location, location. On the Internet, location no longer matters; competition is merely a click away. This creates a switching dilemma in which the customer can find a new supplier relatively easily. For consumers, there are bots that search the Web for lower prices. For firms, there are online exchanges such as FreeMarkets (which, as of late 2000, had accumulated over $10 billion in transactions) in which members can request supplier bids and conduct auctions. For sellers, retention rates may be far lower than those that were prevalent when search costs were significantly higher. Lower retention rates mean lower customer equity.

In the online economy, sellers must concentrate on how to increase switching costs. The best example is the airline industry. Despite questionable on-time reliability and poor customer service, airlines still have been able to foster high loyalty. They have accomplished this through barriers to exit. Frequent-flyer programs, for example, peg the customer's status in the next year to mileage in the current year. Consumer-products firms use a similar mechanism with retailers: Next year's promotional funds depend on this year's orders. Barriers to exit and other mechanisms that increase the customer's cost of switching are going to play a more significant role in customer equity management for online firms.

Of course, traditional strategies also can reduce switching. Customers in the online economy still expect services such as delivery, in-stock items, and other outputs that customers purchasing from traditional channels receive. Amazon.com's success can be attributed in part to its service levels. The company regularly updates the customer when a product is out of stock, and it delivers when it promises to. Catalog retailers have learned how important these services are, and the online economy is no different. E-tailers are expected to provide on-time deliveries and reasonable return and communication policies. When eToys was unable to meet customer expectations about deliveries during the 1999 Christmas season, it led to significant problems for them regarding future customer loyalty.

Branding is a traditional tool designed to decrease switching. Because of the ease with which customers can search for and find substitutes on the Internet, strong brands are even more important now.

Shapiro and Varian provide a very good overview of "lock-in," or what we call barriers to exit. They focus primarily on switching costs and offer several rules that serve as an excellent summary:[3]

- Keep control of information and databases.

- Create brand-specific training.

- As a supplier, switching costs relative to customer revenue are key to valuing your installed base.

- To understand lock-in, look ahead and reason back.

  We have added several other rules to their list:

- Use loyalty programs that provide benefits based on past purchasing.

- Recognize the importance of service outputs if you are a channel.

- Build the brand for your product or service.

### Does the Customer-Information Advantage Win Out?

A critical issue that faces firms in the online world is, Can my company use information to develop a competitive advantage, or will everyone be at parity? It is commonly believed that information on customer behavior can create barriers to entry and can create competitive advantage, but how will this work in a world in which switching costs are relatively low?

One solution is to create an adaptive marketing system, one in which the firm's data about a customer allows it to improve its marketing tactics as more information becomes available. The concept is that each additional purchase or piece of information improves the firm's knowledge of the customer. This, in turn, leads to changing the marketing mix directed at the customer, particularly through product and promotional offers. As the customer responds to the offers, the system continues to learn and to improve.

Two data analysis methods, collaborative filtering and hierarchical Bayesian updating, capitalize on this principle. Collaborative filtering processes customer behavioral information and uses what it finds to recommend products or services for add-on selling. It is a data-driven technique that predicts what a customer might want by analyzing the similarities in purchase behaviors among large groups of customers. The bottom line is that customers have less incentive to switch, because the firm can more efficiently anticipate their needs and preferences.

Hierarchical Bayes models work in a similar manner to collaborative filtering, but they look at factors beyond product offerings, such as pricing, customer service, and promotions. They link causal and behavioral data to recommend marketing-mix elements at the individual-customer level. By tailoring the marketing mix to the individual, the firm can more accurately provide value drivers for the customer, and hence combat switching.

### Whose Customer Is It, Anyway?

The final issue in an online economy is the question of who owns the customer—the channel or the manufacturer? As customers develop relationships with online channel members, it may be the channels, and not the manufacturers, that wield control. If a customer is loyal to AOL, not to its suppliers, and if AOL changes suppliers, the customer will not change channels. The result is that the channel member can dictate terms to the supplier.

To avoid this problem, the manufacturer or supplier must develop strong brand equity. Tide is unlikely to be discontinued at Wal-Mart, because it has very strong brand equity. Purex is in a much weaker position. Therefore, as we have stated, branding is very important for suppliers to e-tailers. Without a strong brand, the channel member can decide not to stock the product.

Channel members, for their part, need to develop strong relationships with customers. When a brand is strong, the customer will change channel members to find the brand it wants at a lower price. Thus, channel members must concentrate on how to provide the value,

service, and other outputs—including variety, convenience, and reliability—demanded by the customer.

In many ways, the online economy is very much like the old one
when it comes to the battle for the customer. The difference is that
because of low switching costs, the battle is more intense than in the
typical channel–supplier power struggle.

## Outsourcing and Strategic Alliances

Of the various managerial and organizational trends that customer
equity–based companies need to address, two will have the greatest
impact in coming years: outsourcing and the development of alliance
networks.

### *Outsourcing*

The trend toward outsourcing is well established. As more and more
companies reengineer, downsize, and reorganize around "core processes,"
they are tempted to outsource every activity in which benchmarking
consultants deem them to be "subscale." EDS, CSC, and others have
built an industry on this in the data processing realm. Accenture (for-
merly Andersen Consulting) and EDS's A.T. Kearney arm, among others, seem headed toward capabilities that will allow companies to outsource just about any managerial or operational task, including
procurement, logistics, and billing and payments.

As we discussed in chapter 5 on add-on selling, "not invented here"
attitudes can limit a firm's ability to enhance its product and service
offerings. Of course, outsourcing can provide many benefits: reduced
cost through the outside provider's scale economies; the opportunity to
focus on critical activities; and increased capital availability, particularly
in areas such as computing, for which the outsourcing company invests
in the hardware. The risks lie in becoming myopically cost driven and
in failing to consider whether outsourced activities limit the firm's ability to maximize customer equity.

What capabilities, then, should customer equity companies never
outsource? First of all, they should never outsource any activity that
involves extracting proprietary insights about consumer behavior from
databases. It is fine to let others crunch numbers, and even to license
access to some data to noncompetitors, but the skills for developing and
testing hypotheses about how customers and prospects behave should

remain in-house. A nonbank credit card issuer learned this lesson the hard way. It retained an external vendor both to analyze household behavioral data and to develop the algorithms with which to do so. Over time, the vendor built tremendous expertise in understanding the behavior and spending patterns of financial-services users, which it then used—naturally enough—to provide similar insights and services to the company's competitors.

This same lesson applies to customer-relationship valuation: The one who learns how to develop the insights gains power over those who simply use the answers. It is true for customer life cycle management, as well. It may be okay to let other people run call centers and mailing programs, but because a considerable measure of customer equity derives from understanding where specific customers are in their relationship life cycles, and from adjusting pricing, retention, and activation programs accordingly, it would be folly to let others run the life cycle engine. Even in the case of outsourced call centers, companies need to put processes in place to ensure that they are not kept from hearing the customer's voice.

The final competence to avoid outsourcing is customer portfolio management. As discussed earlier in the book, companies must manage a mix of acquisition, retention, and add-on selling in all but the most extreme pure plays. Competitive advantage comes from managing the relationship portfolio with more precise targeting and with greater efficiency than competitors do. This crucial task should not fall to outsiders.

In short, it is fine to delegate the donkeywork of data collection and management and of customer-relationship servicing. However, by no means should companies assign to others activities that generate unique insights or that involve massaging the business model to match customer life cycles or portfolios.

### *Alliance Networks*

In a way, the alliance network, or "virtual corporation" phenomenon, is a natural extension of outsourcing. The alliance network principle is somewhat more elegant, however, in that it suggests a value-creating network of relationships (many of which are temporary rather than permanent) that delivers specific benefits to a market or segment. With the blurring of industry boundaries accelerating (where does banking stop and retailing begin?), the most effective customer equity organizations will be those that can meet customer needs by bringing together coalitions of companies without ceding control of customer data and interactions. These networks can be incredibly complex, and they can lead to confusing roles. Companies that compete bitterly in some areas can become allies, customers, or suppliers in other areas.

The emergence of alliance networks has several implications for the elements of customer equity. With regard to acquisition, companies should use access to customers and to behavioral data as a key criterion of alliance attractiveness. Extracting retention value from alliance networks will depend on occupying nodes where streams of customer information come together. In terms of add-on selling, a carefully selected and managed network can create the appearance of a broad, integrated product and service offering without the cost of building one in-house.

Over and above all this, companies need to keep in mind that each member of an alliance network has its own motivations. Many people have noted that in alliance situations the preeminent goal should be to learn faster than your partners do. Before entering into alliance agreements, a company should set its own learning agenda in the context of building customer equity. It also should understand the possible learning agendas of its proposed partners, and how those agendas might endanger its customer equity.

In the alliance game, the bottom line is this: Success depends on access to customer behavioral data, the ability to transform those data into insight, and the customer access necessary to act on that insight. This will become more and more true as customer equity management's basic tools, such as database software, become broadly available and more widely used.

## New Valuations

Through the system of customer equity measurement, firms will be able to value customers, not just traditional assets. This new valuation is controversial and not yet widely accepted. As we indicated early in the book, many Internet companies, particularly e-tailers, are valued on the basis of computations similar to those for customer equity. However, market analysts' poor understanding of how to make these valuations, coupled with the desire to make buy recommendations, has led to absurdly high valuations on a per-customer basis. Now analysts who have been dead wrong in their initial valuations want to throw the baby out with the bath water. They blame the method, not the exuberance.

We can quibble about whether the current market values are reasonable evaluations, but not about the method of valuing customer equity. A stock price can too aggressively assume a customer value. Clearly, someone skilled in the art of customer valuation can provide much more accurate estimates. In earlier chapters we discussed sophisticated analysis methods, such as add-on selling regression-based models and cash flow projection models using survival functions. These methods require expertise beyond that of an analyst who does a back-of-the-envelope calculation. One cannot condemn those using well-designed methods because analyst valuations have been overzealous and underinformed.

We believe that the new method of valuing firms will become standard across many industries and that there are many firms with customer value that the market has not identified. For example, a traditional grocery retailer is likely to have very little customer value built directly into its valuation. Its market valuation is based on growth rates and P/E ratios, not the potential to tap a large customer base. But assume that a retailer with 1,500 stores in the United States has 10,000 customers per store. Research on frequent-shopper cards shows that a typical customer is worth approximately $300 per year and has a lifetime value of $1,200. If we apply these numbers to our grocery retailer, then its customer valuation comes to approximately $18 billion!

Generally such retailers do not have this level of valuation. Why? Because they have failed to follow the model that Amazon.com and AOL have followed, which is based on increasing customer equity. These two companies have recognized that the customer has untapped value and that this value is not captured unless one understands add-on selling. Amazon first sold books, then CDs, and now it sells electronics, computer peripherals, DVDs, and much more. In other words, the customer equity model can lead to greater customer value if the firm understands how to apply it as a business model. Many traditional retailers and old-economy industrial firms have failed to recognize this model. Some understood it long before it was in vogue, including IBM, which created add-on selling (they called it installed-base selling) as a cornerstone of its sales strategy.

## Branding Equity and Customer Equity

Customer equity does not preclude developing strong brands. A firm can have high or low brand equity and high or low customer equity. Obviously, having low customer equity and low brand equity is not desirable. Alternatively, a firm could have high brand equity (a well-known brand) combined with low customer equity because it lacks a quality product or service. Examples of the latter include telecom and credit card companies that have well-known brands but difficulty in differentiating their products and services from those of the competition. Local electric utilities are starting to face the same problem as deregulation kicks in.

Obviously, high customer equity and high brand equity is a desirable combination. But a firm should consider whether investing in a brand will increase its value if it already has high customer equity. In other words, the cost of attaining high brand equity may be greater than the potential benefit.

High customer equity can create high brand equity. USAA, an insurance company, is an example of a firm that did not aggressively advertise or market its brand; through superior service and great value, however, it built a cadre of policyholders willing to buy anything USAA would sell. It had the lowest acquisition costs in the insurance industry, and it was able to easily sell add-on products and services. Yet it did not have strong brand equity. Only those who were policyholders really knew it existed. It was not a household name, like Lloyds of London or Allstate, but it built significantly higher customer equity per customer.

In an online economy, will brand equity become more important than customer equity? Obviously, both will be important, but we will make predictions based on the following reasonable assumptions:

- The online economy has far less friction (difficulty changing suppliers) than the traditional economy does.

- Customers require information regarding products and services and do not have 100 percent awareness of all substitutes.

- There will be information tools that make product information far more available.

- Customer service will continue to be at a premium.

In this world there will be a basic rule: Those companies one step removed in the channel must develop brand equity first, and customer equity will follow. Those that are directly connected to the customer must create customer equity first, and brand equity will follow. Firms whose products are sold through a channel will have far more difficulty creating customer equity, whereas those directly connected to customers will be much more vulnerable if they have low customer equity.

## Privacy Concerns

We have saved the potentially most damaging phenomenon, increasing privacy concerns, for last. The backlash against intrusions into consumer privacy has been underway for the last decade. One example of this comes from the Netherlands, where the Ahold supermarket chain instituted a loyalty card program and began targeted marketing efforts based on purchase data. Subsequently, some consumers set up a Web site where Ahold customers could exchange loyalty cards with each other, ostensibly to garner the discounts available to cardholders while scrambling the individual behavioral data available to Ahold.

Clearly, for a vocal minority, limiting access to customer data is a fighting cause. But whether they object or not, all consumers are beginning to understand that information about themselves has value to others. If customer equity management depends on the steady flow of customer data, this developing awareness deserves some thought.

Will consumer fears of Big Brother doom the effectiveness of customer equity approaches? It is very possible that some types of customer data will prove harder to obtain and that government regulation will tightly restrict access to certain household financial data. Companies may even find themselves locked out from customer information that is readily available today.

Even in such an environment, however, there are steps that customer equity–based companies can take to maximize their customer relationships and to obtain the most data possible. First, companies should adopt strategies that reward customers with services, or even with goods or cash, for the information access that they cede. Witness Mercedes-Benz, which places customers on the mailing list for its "private" magazine and invites them to special events in exchange for the completion of an annual survey. Of course, the cost of such rewards needs to be balanced against the contribution that the information they garner makes to a company's acquisition, retention, or add-on selling strategies.

Second, companies need to be honest with themselves and with their customers about their intentions. Creating and living by a code of conduct for the use of customer information is one option, though not the only one. On a more general level, companies must commit to maximizing not only the value that they receive from their customer relationships, but also the value that their customers receive from them. Give value, gain trust. As trust grows, privacy issues likely will become less significant.

Privacy concerns have repercussions for each element of customer equity. Especially during the acquisition process, companies should realize that customer information carries a price. There is good news, however, for retention strategies. In a world of constrained information access, those who create value for their customers, and in doing so gain customers' trust along with access to their proprietary information, will have the opportunity to build significant switching barriers. Similarly, this incumbent status as a provider should confer advantages to a company's add-on selling activities. In fact, privacy is one of the few forces that tend to significantly increase the viability of add-on selling as a core strategy.

By the same token, however, companies probably will face restrictions on sharing customer information with partners, which means that some of the approaches discussed earlier that involve alliances and virtual bundled offerings may become less viable.

## Getting Current—Then Moving Ahead

We understand that the concepts of customer equity described in this book are well ahead of the existing practices in most industries and businesses. Even so, we hope that the warning of this chapter is clear: With the pace of change you face today, catching up will not be enough. Or, on a more optimistic note: If you can jump all the way to using customer equity as it will exist in the future, and change the rules of the game for your competitors as a result, you'll be very, very difficult to catch.

# APPENDIX
## *Issues in Computing Customer Equity*

As firms perfect their customer equity computation, six basic issues generally arise:

1. What time horizon to use in projecting sales and other data

2. What time periods to measure

3. Which cohorts to select

4. Which level of approximation to use for accounting and financial numbers

5. What data are required

6. How to handle missing data

### Time Horizon

One of the most controversial questions to decide in measuring customer equity is how far into the future to project sales and retention rates. The longer the projection, the greater the total customer equity, but the less certain the findings.

Using a relatively high discount rate in the computations solves part of this problem. High discount rates mean that future profits receive very little value. For example, with a discount rate of 20 percent, discounted profits ten years into the future are multiplied by

$(1/1.2)^{10}$, or 0.162. Still, even this relatively low value adds significantly to customer equity when accumulated over another ten years.

Another option is setting a finite time horizon of only five to ten years, which limits the uncertainty that comes with longer-term projections. However, this method may lead businesses whose customers typically last longer than five or ten years to underestimate their customers' future value.

We recommend projecting customer equity over a long time horizon while using a high discount rate to reflect the uncertainty of future customer revenue streams. This emphasizes current profits in the equation, but it does not penalize a firm that has customers who last twenty to thirty years.

### Time Periods for Measurement

Sales, profit, and retention rate data can be compiled on a yearly, quarterly, or other periodic basis. It is most common to track these data on a yearly basis. However, one year may be too long for certain types of businesses. For example, in the clothing catalog industry, firms tend to follow a six-month marketing cycle, mailing out catalogs in the spring and fall. For them, a six-month tracking period works best. Consumer packaged-goods retailers, such as mass merchants, chain drug stores, and grocery stores, often have very rapid purchase cycles, as short as one to three weeks. These businesses may be better off compiling their data by month or by quarter.

We generally recommend time periods of one year or less, particularly if the firm's product or service has a short purchase cycle, along with separate measurement of purchase or sale rates per period. We also strongly recommend measuring silent attrition, which will give a much better idea of the overall retention picture. For example, without measuring silent attrition, it could appear that a firm has a high retention rate and low purchase rate when in fact the problem is just the opposite.

### Customer Cohorts

As firms move from computing the equity of a single customer to computing the equity of a customer segment or the entire database, the issue of grouping customers into cohorts for analysis becomes salient. A cohort is a set of customers acquired in the same time period, such as a given month or year. Analysts can compute various customer equity probabilities and financial calculations using samples taken from the cohort. The more similar the customers in the cohort are to each other, the more representative the samples and the resulting statistics. Sample size is also critical, because as the number of time periods included in a customer equity analysis increases, the number of retained customers generally decreases. For the purposes of this kind of statistical analysis, a minimum sample size of thirty is recommended for analyses of more than five or ten years. (A sample size of thirty is considered a large sample. This number comes from various statistical tables used to approximate normal distribution.)

Customers grouped into a cohort should share several characteristics: the time period in which they began as customers, the method through which they were acquired as customers (e.g., they were acquired through use of a sales force), similar purchase and retention behavior (though obviously it is not required to be identical), and histories long enough to be measurable. In practice, because it is difficult to create an exactly matched cohort, these requirements can be approximately met.

When measuring a company's customer equity, analysts should select several distinct cohorts with a variety of acquisition periods. This allows a firm to gauge how customer equity numbers, such as add-on selling, retention rates, and acquisition costs, change over time.

## *Approximating Accounting and Financial Numbers*

Many accountants and financial analysts argue that customer equity cannot be measured because highly precise accounting numbers do not exist. We beg to differ. Even when exact numbers are absent, it is better to be roughly right and to utilize the concept of customer equity than not to measure it and to operate an enterprise using insufficient indicators, such as current sales and profits. Such indicators may be more accurately measured, but they are less relevant managerially and strategically. Thus it is often necessary to approximate accounting and financial numbers when trying to measure profit levels and marketing expenses for historical cohorts of customers.

## *Data Requirements for Computing Customer Equity*

Customer equity–driven firms need customer databases. An effective database includes a customer identifier used to track all customer activities; customer purchase histories; customer-level causal data; and incremental cost data.

A customer identifier must be a unique identifier. (Physical addresses generally are not the best choice.) The source of the identifier can be a preferred customer card, a credit card, or another type of tracking mechanism. This source needs to capture at least 80 percent of the customer's purchases; if not, conclusions regarding customer behavior may be spurious.

Analysts use customer purchase histories to measure retention rates, sales per customer over time, and acquisition rates. These statistics form the basis for the computation of customer equity.

Causal data by customer comes from tracking marketing communications, special promotions and pricing, and any other relevant marketing activities directed at the customer, such as customer service and returns.

Incremental cost data must be tracked at the customer level. Many firms do not know the true incremental cost of a sale, which includes the costs of goods, warehousing, distribution, and other incremental infrastructure costs. The accounting department must determine these costs if a firm wants to obtain an accurate picture of its customers' profitability.

### Adjusting for Missing Data

Because of the retrospective nature of customer equity computations, data frequently will be missing. Firms rarely collect perfect customer marketing, sales, and cost data, and some firms do not even track customers accurately. As a result, a firm often will need to approximate missing data. The logic behind this is similar to that explained earlier: It is better to be roughly right than to rely on inappropriate but more exact statistical and financial measures.

Among the data most typically lacking are the following: advertising investments over time, by type of objective (e.g., acquisition, retention, or add-on selling); sales force activities by account; customer service activities by account; and incremental costs of products.

# Notes

## Chapter 1

1. Robert A. Burgelman, "The Charles Schwab Corporation in 1996," Case SM-35 (Stanford, CA: Graduate School of Business, Stanford University, 1997).
2. Michael E. Gazala, Bill Doyle, and Shelley Morrisette, "One-Stop Shops Won't Cut It," *The Forrester Report* 3, no. 12 (August 1998).
3. John Thakray, "GM's Global Push," *Management Today*, April 1980, 50–54.
4. Jesse Snyder and Raymond Serifin, "GM to Spend Big to Recover Share," *Advertising Age*, 16 September 1985, 1.
5. Jerry Flint, "The Ghost of Alfred Sloan," *Forbes*, 25 May 1981, 34–38.

## Chapter 2

1. One such article was Robert Blattberg and John Golanty, "Tracker: An Early Test Market Forecasting and Diagnostic Model for New Product Planning," *Journal of Marketing Research* 15 (May 1978): 192–202.

## Chapter 3

1. Jacquelyn S. Thomas, "A Methodology Linking Customer Acquisition to Customer Retention," *Journal of Marketing Research* (forthcoming in 2001).
2. Robert Blattberg, John Deighton, and Jacquelyn Thomas, "Setting the Marketing Mix Maximizing Customer Equity," working paper, Kellogg School of Management, Evanston, IL, 1998.
3. Sam Zuckerman, "E-Trade Loses $5.2 Million Despite Late Business Surge," *San Francisco Chronicle*, 20 January 2000, B2.
4. Tim Jackson, "AOL Merges with the Field," *Financial Times*, 22 December 1997, 9.
5. Ibid.

6. Jacquelyn S. Thomas and Robert Blattberg, "Pricing Based on Customer Relationships," working paper, Stanford University Graduate School of Business, Stanford, CA, 1999.

7. If the firm does not construct completely orthogonal partitions, some buyers will be included in more than one partition. Ideally, the firm should divide the database so that a customer is a member of only one partition.

### Chapter 4

1. Shelly Reese, "Happiness Isn't Everything," *American Demographics*, May 1996, 52–58.

2. Frederick Reichheld, "Learning from Customer Defections," *Harvard Business Review* 74, no. 2 (March–April 1996): 56–69.

3. Michael Lowenstein, "Keep Them Coming Back," *American Demographics*, May 1996, 54–57.

4. P. A. LaBarbera and D. Mazursky, "A Longitudinal Assessment of Consumer Satisfaction/Dissatisfaction: The Dynamic Aspect of the Cognitive Process," *Journal of Marketing Research* 20, no. 11 (1983): 393–404; Roland Rust and Anthony Zahorik, "Customer Satisfaction, Customer Retention, and Market Share," *Journal of Retailing* 69, no. 2 (1993): 193–213.

5. Christine T. Ennew and Martin Binks, "The Impact of Service Quality and Service Characteristics on Customer Retention: Small Businesses and Their Banks in the UK," *British Journal of Management* 7, no. 3 (1996): 219–230.

6. Gerard King, "Achieving Customer Retention through Quality Management and Marketing," *Asian Pacific Journal of Quality Management* 4, no. 2 (1995): 59–61.

7. Susan Keaveney, "Customer Switching Behavior in Service Industries: An Exploratory Study," *Journal of Marketing* 59 (1995): 71–82.

8. Jacquelyn S. Thomas, "A Methodology Linking Customer Acquisition to Customer Retention," *Journal of Marketing Research* (forthcoming in 2001).

9. V. A. Zeithaml, "How Consumer Evaluation Processes Differ Between Goods and Services," in *Marketing of Services*, eds. J. H. Donnelly and W. R. George (Chicago: American Marketing Association, 1981).

10. Patricia Seybold, "Don't Count Out Amazon," *Business 2.0*, 10 October 2000, 99.

11. Jacquelyn S. Thomas and Robert Blattberg, "Pricing Based on Customer Relationships," working paper, Stanford University Graduate School of Business, Stanford, CA, 1999.

12. Frederick Reichheld and W. Earl Sasser Jr., "Zero Defections: Quality Comes to Services," *Harvard Business Review* 68, no. 5 (September–October 1990): 105–111.

13. Mark Van Clieaf, "Identifying Your Most Profitable Customers," *Business Quarterly* 61, no. 2 (1996): 54–60.

14. Robert Blattberg and John Deighton, "Manage Marketing by the Customer Equity Test," *Harvard Business Review* 74, no. 4 (July–August 1996): 136–144.

15. Robert Blattberg, John Deighton, and Jacquelyn Thomas, "Setting the Marketing Mix Maximizing Customer Equity," working paper, Kellogg School of Management, Evanston, IL, 1998.

### Chapter 5

1. Paine-Webber, *Portfolio Manager's Spotlight*, New York, December 1998. Churn, which refers to lost customers, equals 1 minus retention.

2. Jacquelyn S. Thomas and Werner Reinartz, "An Empirical Investigation into the Impact of Cross-Buying on Customer Retention and Customer Lifetime Value," working paper, Goizueta Business School, Atlanta, GA, 2000.

### Chapter 6

1. Robert C. Blattberg, John Deighton, and Jacquelyn Thomas, "Setting the Marketing Mix Maximizing Customer Equity," working paper, Kellogg School of Management, Evanston, IL, 1998.
2. Jacquelyn S. Thomas and Robert C. Blattberg, "Pricing Based on Customer Relationships," working paper, Stanford University Graduate School of Business, Stanford, CA, 1999.
3. Frederick F. Reichheld and W. Earl Sasser Jr., " Zero Defections: Quality Comes to Services," *Harvard Business Review* 68, no. 5 (September–October 1990): 105–111.
4. The margin and expenditure figures used in this computation are per customer.
5. The unit of time for this duration is the same as the unit of time that the retention rate is measured in. For example, if the retention rate is 70 percent per year, the expected relationship duration would be 3.33 years, or $1/(1 - 0.7)$.
6. For the purposes of this example we assume that changes in the add-on buying rate will not increase the customer retention rate. This is counter to the data that are presented in chapter 5.
7. Note that the number of customers each year does not increase by 1,500 because customer churn occurs during the year.

### Chapter 9

1. We do not pretend that this book adds to the extensive literature on conceptual frameworks for organizing; instead, we have selected one of many available frameworks and summarized it briefly here.
2. For a brief discussion of the priority of unspoken rules over spoken ones, see Christopher Meyer, *Fast Cycle Time* (New York: The Free Press, 1993), 64–65.
3. Madhav Srinivasan, "Keeping Your Customers," *Business and Economic Review* 43, no. 1 (1996): 7–11.
4. Ibid.
5. Charles R. Weiser, "Championing the Customer," *Harvard Business Review* 73, no. 6 (November–December 1995): 113–116.
6. Srinivasan, "Keeping Your Customers."
7. Frederick F. Reichheld and W. Earl Sasser Jr., " Zero Defections: Quality Comes to Services," *Harvard Business Review* 68, no. 5 (September–October 1990): 105–111.
8. D'Anne Hotchkiss, "What Do Your Customers Really Think?" *Bank Marketing* 27, no. 3 (1995): 13–20.

### Chapter 10

1. Kelly J. Andrews, "State of the Industry," *Target Marketing* 22, no. 1 (1999): 36–40.
2. Tricia Campbell, "Database Marketing for the Little Guys," *Sales and Marketing Management* 151, no. 6 (1999): 69.
3. Carl Shapiro and Hal R. Varian, *Information Rules* (Boston: Harvard Business School Press, 1999).

# INDEX

Accenture, 201
accounting systems
  customer equity balance sheet,
    163–169
  customer equity flow statement, 10,
    169–171
  decile and RFM analyses, 89–92
  in organizational design, 182–183
  statistical modeling
    of add-on selling, 120, 122–123,
      200
    of customer acquisition, 25, 43, 45,
      59, 62–65
    of customer retention, 27, 92
  *See also* databases
acquisition equity
  at Buford Electronics, 26, 27, 29–30
  measuring and computing, 4, 5,
    56–58
    analysis tools for, 58–59
    profiling in, 60–62
    regression scoring in, 62–65
  optimizing, 31–32
    measurement levers in, 132–137
  *See also* customer acquisition
acquisition margin, 132, 133, 135
acquisition marketing expenditures,
  132, 133, 135

acquisition pricing, 47, 48, 51
acquisition rate, 57, 132, 133, 135
acquisition tactical management. *See*
    ACTMAN acquisition model
acquisition thresholds, 154–156
acquisition transaction and process, 36
ACTMAN acquisition model
  applied to U.S. Armed Forces, 50–52
  generating awareness in, 46–47
  nature of, 42–43, 44, 66
  pricing in, 47–48
  product trials in, 48–49
  targeting in, 43, 45–46
adaptive marketing system
  adjusting expenditures in, 126, 129
  adjusting prices in, 129–130
  databases in, 131–132
  with e-commerce, 199–200
  nature of, 126, 127–128
add-on buying rate, 132, 133, 135, 136
add-on offers, 103, 105, 109
add-on selling
  aligning acquisition and retention
    with, 35–36, 38, 39, 58, 75, 82
  customer affinity in, 108–111
  defined, 95–96
  determining firm value in, 103,
    105–108

add-on selling *(continued)*
  in developing customer equity, 11,
    12, 24
  future forces driving, 194–195, 200,
    201, 202, 203, 204, 207
  make-or-buy decision for, 115–117
  marketing strategies and mix for,
    147, 159–160
    during customer life cycle, 148,
      149–150
    industry thresholds in, 154,
      158–159
  methods and tools for, 21, 119–123
    customer equity balance sheet,
      163–169
    customer equity flow statement,
      169–171
  Oprah Winfrey and, 112–115
  optimizing, 125–126
    adaptive marketing in, 126,
      128–132
    at Donelson & Ward, 137–144
    measurement levers in, 132–137
  in organizational design, 176–179,
    180, 190–191
  products and services in, 96–97, 98
  retention rates and customer value
    in, 117–119
  role and impact of, 96
  at Sports Expert Online, 97, 99–103,
    104
add-on selling equity
  accounting and computing,
    119–120
    collaborative filtering in, 122
    cross-buying analysis in, 121–122
    response modeling in, 122–123
  benefits of computing, 4, 5
  optimizing, 31–32
    measurement levers in, 132–137
add-on selling margin, 108, 132, 135
add-on selling marketing expenditures,
  132, 135
advertising
  acquiring customers with TV, 46,
    50–51
  adaptive marketing for Internet, 126,
    127
  in building customer affinity, 6–7

marketing mix in, 159–160
  through customer life cycle,
    148–154
Aeroquip, 74
Ahold supermarket chain, 206
Air Force, 50, 51. *See also* U.S. Armed
  Forces
airline industry
  add-on selling in, 110
  customer retention in, 70, 84–85,
    155, 157
  organizational design for customer
    equity in, 184, 185, 188
  switching barriers in, 198
alliance networks, 194, 202–203
Amazon Anywhere, 78
Amazon.com, 49, 96, 122, 181, 199, 204
  customer retention at, 75–80
Amazon Wish List, 78
AMD, 158
American Express Membership
  Rewards, 40–42
America Online (AOL), 37, 46, 115,
  161–162, 200, 204
Andersen Consulting. *See* Accenture
ARA marketing model
  customer life cycle in, 148–154
  industry thresholds in, 154–155
    acquisition, 155–156
    add-on selling, 158–159
    retention, 157–158
  nature of, 147, 159–160
Army, 50. *See also* U.S. Armed Forces
A. T. Kearney, 176, 201
AT&T, 96
attitudinal data, 54–55
attrition, 69. *See also* core defectors
automobile industry
  customer acquisition in, 49
  customer retention in, 71, 85
  maximizing customer asset value in,
    5–6
awareness generation, 46–47
  Armed Forces campaigns for, 50–51

Baldrige competition, 71
banking industry. *See* financial services
  industry

barriers to exit. *See* switching barriers
beliefs, organizational, 174, 187–189
*Blown to Bits* (Evans and Wurster), 77
Bluefly.com, 165, 166–169
brand equity, 6–7, 205–206
brand marketing
  in add-on selling, 129
  for customer affinity, 108–109
  in customer equity management, 3, 4
  effects of organizational design on,
    175, 181–182, 191
  future of, 197, 199, 200
  in segmentation, targeting, and posi-
    tioning, 147
British Airways, 184, 185, 188
brokerage industry. *See* financial serv-
    ices industry
Buford Electronics, 25–30

Cap Gemini, 176
CARESS (Customer Analysis and
    Retention System), 184, 188
causal marketing databases, 55–56, 119,
    211, 212
channels of distribution, 7
  in e-commerce, 200–201
  in marketing mix, 150, 159–160
Charles Schwab, 4
Christensen, Clayton, 77
Citibank, 96
Coast Guard, 50. *See also* U.S. Armed
    Forces
cohorts
  computing and analyzing, 210–211
  defined, 163–164
collaborative filtering, 120, 122, 200
Compaq, 37–38
computer industry
  add-on selling in, 95, 96, 108, 110
  customer acquisition in, 37
  customer retention in, 157–158
  organizational design for customer
    equity in, 176
consumer-products firms
  add-on selling in, 106, 108
  organizational design for customer
    equity in, 175
core competencies, 109–110

core customers
  in customer life cycle, 14, 16, 18, 19,
    20
  marketing to, 151, 153–154
core defectors
  attrition and, 69
  in customer life cycle, 14, 16, 18, 19
  flow statement in targeting,
    170–171
  marketing to, 151, 153–154
  RS matrix in targeting, 91–92
  statistical models in predicting, 92
credit card companies
  in acquiring customers, 37, 53–54
  brand equity in, 205
  outsourcing by, 202
  use of databases by, 21
cross-buying, 118–119
  analysis, 120, 121–122
cross-functional teams, 177, 179–181,
    185
cross-purchase analysis, 119, 120
cross-selling, 6, 10, 95–96, 119
CSC, 176, 201
customer acquisition
  ACTMAN model of, 42–43
    awareness generation and position-
      ing in, 46–47
    pricing of product or service in,
      47–48
    product experience and satisfaction
      in, 49
    target marketing in, 43–44
    trials in, 48–49
  aligning retention and add-on selling
    with, 35–36, 71–72, 80, 81–82
  American Express Membership
    Rewards for, 40–42
  defined, 36
  in developing customer equity, 11,
    12, 24, 25–30
  future forces driving, 194–195, 202,
    207
  industries focused on, 36–37
  marketing strategies and mix for,
    147, 159–160
    during customer life cycle,
      149–150
    industry thresholds, 154–156

customer acquisition *(continued)*
  methods and tools for, 52
    customer equity balance sheet,
      163–169
    customer equity flow statement,
      169–171
    databases, 21, 52–56
    measuring and accounting, 56–58,
      211
    profiling and regression scoring,
      58–65
  optimizing, 125–126
    adaptive marketing in, 126,
      128–132
    at Donelson & Ward, 137–144
    measurement levers in, 132–137
    rules for, 38–40
  in organizational design, 176–179,
    180, 189–191
  selective, 37–38
  by U.S. Armed Forces, 50–52
  *See also* acquisition equity
customer affinity
  in add-on selling, 108–109, 158
  delivering on expectations for,
    110–111
  managing, 111
    Oprah Winfrey in, 113–114
  in maximizing customer asset value,
    6–7
  recognizable expertise for, 109–110
customer development management
    teams (CDMTs), 180–181, 185
customer equity
  balance sheet of, 163–166
    at Bluefly.com, 166–169
  benefits of, 4–5
  computing and quantifying, 22–24
    at Buford Electronics, 25–30
    cohorts in, 210–211
    data requirements in, 211–212
    missing data in, 212
    models of marketing mix in,
      24–25
    technology in, 7–8
    time horizon in, 209–210
    time periods in, 210
  flow statement measurement of, 10,
    169–171

future of, 193, 194–195, 207
  brand equity in, 205–206
  customer and firm valuations in,
    203–204
  customer privacy in, 206–207
  e-commerce in, 197–201
  outsourcing and alliances in,
    201–203
  technological advances in, 193,
    196–197
marketing focus of, 147, 159–160
  changes and trends in, 8–10
  criteria of system performance in, 12
  industry thresholds in, 154–159
  through life cycle stages, 148–154
nature of managing, 3–4, 13–14
optimizing and balancing, 31–32, 85,
  125–126
  adaptive marketing system in,
    126–132
  Donelson & Ward in, 137–144
  fundamental measurement levers
    in, 132–137
stages of customer life cycle in, 14–16
  analysis of, 17–18
  at Zap Online, 19–20
customer equity balance sheet
  of Bluefly.com, 166–169
  elements of, 163–165
customer equity equation, 23–24
customer equity flow statement, 10,
  169–171
customer expectations
  in add-on selling, 110–111, 114
  in customer retention, 72, 79, 84
customer identifiers, 211–212
customer interaction databases, 84–85,
  86
customer life cycle
  managing, 3, 5, 13–14
  measuring, 16–18
  stages of, 14–16
  at Zap Online, 19–20
customer management quiz, xvii–xix
customer purchase histories, 211, 212
customer retention
  aligning acquisition and add-on sell-
    ing with, 35–36, 38–40, 58, 66,
    81–82

at Amazon.com, 75–80
changing retention rates in, 80–81
defined, 68–69
determinants of, 71–75
in developing customer equity, 11,
    12, 24, 25, 27–30
future forces driving, 194–195, 202,
    203, 207
in grocery industry, 67–68
industries with low and high, 36–37
marketing strategies and mix for,
    147, 159–160
  during customer life cycle,
      149–150
  industry thresholds, 154–155,
      157–158
methods and tools for, 210, 211
  customer equity balance sheet,
      163–169
  customer equity flow statement,
      169–171
  databases, 21, 84–85
  decile and FRM analyses, 89–91
  measuring and accounting, 85–88
  in targeting defectors, 91–92
myths about, 69–71
optimizing, 125–126
  adaptive marketing in, 126,
      128–132
  at Donelson & Ward, 137–144
  measurement levers in, 132–137
in organizational design, 176–179,
    180, 190–191
pricing in, 47–48, 83–84
retention spending in, 82–83
*See also* retention equity
customer satisfaction
in add-on selling, 97
in retaining customers, 71, 75, 84,
    157
*See also* customer value
customer value
in add-on selling, 117–119
computing, 4, 5
  equation for, 23–24
in managing customer equity, 13,
    22–23
in organizational design, 188
*See also* customer satisfaction

databases
in adaptive marketing, 131–132
in add-on selling, 106, 108, 119
in ARA marketing model, 158,
    159–160
in customer acquisition, 52–56
in customer cohort analysis, 210–211
in customer retention, 84–85
future technology of, 196
in managing customer equity, 7–8,
    13, 149, 182, 185, 186
in targeting and analyzing customer
    equity, 21–22, 211–212
*See also* accounting systems
data processing outsourcing, 201
data storage, 196
decile analysis, 64, 89
decision calculus procedure, 87
defections. *See* core defectors
delivered quality, 72, 79
Dell, 37–38, 108
demographic data, 45, 53, 60, 61
Department of Defense, 50, 51
depth of repeat, 17, 18
diminishing returns principle, 38
disintermediation, 195
distribution channels. *See* channels of
    distribution
divest/restructure acquisition, 40
Donelson & Ward, 137–144
Dun & Bradstreet, 60, 64
duration-adjusted retention rates, 88

early repeat buyers
in customer life cycle, 14, 15, 18, 19
marketing to, 151, 152–153
e-commerce
brand equity with, 205–206
impact of, on customer equity, 193,
    194, 197–198
information advantage with, 199–200
switching dilemma with, 198–199
eConvergent, 79
EDS, 176, 201
electric utilities industry, brand equity
    in, 205
electronics components industry, cus-
    tomer equity in, 25–30

employees
measuring performance of, 183–184
organizational functions of, 174,
186–189
support systems for, 184–185
technological skills of, 196–197
Ernst & Young, 176
eToys, 199
Evans, Philip, 77
exit barriers. *See* switching barriers

Federal Drug Administration, 156
Federal Express, 109, 110, 155, 157
Fidelity, 4, 184–185, 188
"Financial Freedom" (Orman), 114
financial services industry
add-on selling in, 96, 158
customer acquisition in, 37, 154
customer retention in, 68
organizational design for customer
equity in, 184–185, 188, 189
outsourcing in, 202
understanding customer needs in, 4
First American Bank Corporation, 189
first-degree targeting, 21, 43, 45–46, 51
First Horizon Bank, 96
First Tennessee Bank, 96
first-time buyers
in customer life cycle, 14, 15, 18, 19
marketing to, 151, 152
FreeMarkets, 198
full throttle acquisition, 39, 40

Gemini Consulting, 176
General Motors (GM), 5–6, 49
Gillette, 179
grocery industry
company and customer valuations in,
204
consumer privacy in, 206
customer retention in, 67–68
use of databases in, 21

Harpo Productions, 114
hierarchical Bayes analysis, 200
hotel industry, use of databases in, 21
H2 blockers, 156

IBM, 95, 204
incremental cost data, 211, 212
individual-customer targeting, 21, 43,
45–46, 51
information systems. *See* accounting
systems; databases
*Innovator's Dilemma, The* (Christensen),
77
installed-base selling, 95, 204
insurance industry, brand equity in, 205
Intel, 157–158
interaction databases, 84–85, 86
Internet advertising, 126
Internet brands, 181–182
Internet companies
in acquiring customers, 37, 46, 49
add-on selling by, 96, 115, 121–122
customer equity accounting by,
161–162, 165, 166–169
in optimizing customer equity, 31
in providing services and products,
199, 200
in retaining customers, 75–80
use of databases by, 21
valuations of, 203–204
*See also* e-commerce
Internet service providers
add-on selling by, 115
in managing customer life cycle,
19–20
introductory pricing, 47, 48

Japanese automobile industry
customer asset value in, 6
customer retention in, 85
Johnson & Johnson Credo, 174
Junior Reserve Officer Training Corps
(JROTC), 51

Kotler, Philip, 46

leadership behavior, 174–175, 189.
*See also* management
L&E Incorporated, 100, 101–102
Lewis, Michael, 77
Lexus, 85
*Life*, 111

lifestyle clusters, 45
lifetime value of a customer, 85. *See also* retention equity
lock-in barriers, 199. *See also* switching barriers
logit models, 25, 92, 120, 122
log-linear models, 120
long-run prices, 48
loyalty mechanisms
at Amazon.com, 77–78
in retaining customers, 70, 72, 73

magazine business
adaptive marketing in, 130
add-on selling in, 112–115
*See also* publishing industry
make-or-buy decision, 105, 115–117
management
benefits and assets of customer equity, 4–5
in customer equity organizational design, 174–175
analytical and technical skills of, 186–187
beliefs and leadership qualities of, 187–189
imperatives of, 175–177, 189–191
structure of, 177–182
marketing focus in, 5–7
changes and trends of, 8–10
nature of customer equity, 3–4
systems and processes, 174, 182–185
technological capabilities for, 7–8
Marines, 50. *See also* U.S. Armed Forces
marketing
adaptive, 126–128
adjusting expenditures in, 126, 129
adjusting prices in, 129–130
databases in, 131–132
ARA model of, 147, 159–160
industry thresholds in, 154–159
stages of customer life cycle in, 148–154
changes and trends in customer, 8–10
criteria of customer equity system, 12
customer equity approach to, 3–4
model of, 10–11
in managing customer life cycle, 14–15, 19–20

maximizing customer as asset in, 4–5
mix in computing customer value, 24–25
technology in analyzing customer, 7–8
use of databases in, 21–22
mass marketing, 9, 10, 46
matchmakers, 115. *See also* make-or-buy decision
MBNA, 179
McGraw, Phil, 114
MCI Friends and Family, 91
Mercedes-Benz, 206
Merrill Lynch, 154
Microsoft, 110
Microsoft Excel, 137
Moore's Law, 193, 196
MotherNature.com, 31
MyCatalog, 166

Navy, 50. *See also* U.S. Armed Forces
Neiman-Marcus, 73
net present value (NPV)
in customer acquisition, 38, 39, 40, 57–58
in customer retention, 75–76, 88
Donelson & Ward in optimizing, 142–143
neural nets, 120
*New New Thing, The* (Lewis), 77
new-product acceptance models, 16, 17

*O* magazine, 112–115
one-on-one marketing, 21–22, 115
online economy. *See* e-commerce; Internet companies
online exchanges, 198
Oprah.com, 113, 115
Oprah's Book Club, 114, 115
*The Oprah Show*, 113, 114
organizational design
customer equity belief system in, 187–189
customer equity imperatives in, 175–177, 189–191
customer equity principles of, 173–175

organizational design *(continued)*
    customer equity structures in,
        177–181
        department roles in, 181–182
    customer equity systems and
        processes in, 182–185
    employees with customer equity
        skills in, 186–187
original equipment manufacturers
    (OEMs), 116
Orman, Suze, 114
outsourcing
    in add-on selling, 116–117
    alliance networks as extensions of,
        202–203
    trends and companies in, 94, 176,
        201–202
Oxygen Media, 114


pay as you go acquisition, 40
penetration pricing, 47
people. *See* employees; management
Pepcid, 156
Pets.com, 31
pharmaceutical industry
    customer acquisition in, 60–61
    marketing strategies and mix in, 156
    organizational design for customer
        equity in, 180
positioning, 46–47
pricing
    in adaptive marketing, 129–130
    in customer acquisition, 45, 47–48,
        51
        effects of trial on, 48–49
    in customer retention, 70, 81, 83–84
    marketing mix in, 159–160
        through customer life cycle,
            148–154
privacy, 193, 195, 206–207
Procter & Gamble, 106, 108
products
    adaptive marketing of, 129, 130
    in ARA marketing model, 148–154,
        159–160
    in fostering customer life cycle,
        14–17
    in maximizing customer asset value,
        6–7

    in promoting add-on selling, 96–97,
        98
        customer affinity and, 113, 114
        make-or-buy decisions regarding,
            115–117, 121–122
        offers, responses, and marketing of,
            105–108
    in promoting customer acquisition,
        49, 156
    in promoting customer retention,
        72–75, 157–158
        at Amazon.com, 79–80
profile databases
    in customer acquisition, 43, 53–55,
        59, 60–62
    nature of, 185
promotions
    marketing mix in, 159–160
        through customer life cycle,
            148–154
    in maximizing customer asset value,
        6–7
prospects
    in customer life cycle, 12, 14–15, 20
    databases in acquiring, 52–53, 56, 64,
        65
    marketing to, 148, 151, 152
publishing industry
    adaptive marketing in, 130
    add-on selling in, 97, 99–103, 104,
        111, 112–115
    customer acquisition in, 55
purchase cycles
    ease of, 73, 78
    effects of, on add-on selling, 119
    effects of, on customer acquisition, 156
    effects of, on customer retention,
        68–69
    RFM analysis in calculating, 89–91
pure type organizations, 189–191.
        *See also* organizational design


reacquired customers, 47
recency, frequency, and monetary
        model. *See* RFM analysis
recency-sales rate (RS) matrix, 91–92
reference value, 91
regression analysis, 27, 120, 122–123,
        200. *See also* regression scoring

regression scoring, 43, 45, 59, 62–65
Reserve Officer Training Corps
    (ROTC), 51
response modeling, 120, 122–123
response rates, determining, 105–106,
    107, 109
restructured acquisition strategy, 40
retail industry
    add-on selling in, 108, 121–122
    customer equity balance sheet in,
        166–169
    customer retention in, 73
    e-commerce and customer equity in,
        199
retention equity
    in analyzing customer life cycle, 17
    at Buford Electronics, 27, 28, 29–30
    marketing mix in changing, 24–25
    measuring and calculating, 4, 5,
        85–86, 87–88
        RFM model in, 87
        survival model in, 86–87
    optimizing, 31–32
        measurement levers in, 132–137
    *See also* customer retention
retention margin, 132, 135
retention marketing expenditures, 132,
    137
retention pricing, 48
retention rate, 132–135
retention spending, 80–81, 82–83
retention thresholds, 154–155,
    157–158
rewards
    in motivating employees, 183–184
    in retaining customers, 73, 75, 77, 78
RFM analysis
    in computing customer life cycle, 16,
        17–18
    in computing retention equity, 86, 87
    in predicting future customer pur-
        chases, 89–91
RS matrix, 91–92

Salon.com, 69
San Francisco 49ers, 99
San Francisco Giants, 99
Schwab, 4
Sears, 108

second-degree (segmented) targeting,
    43, 45
segmentation, targeting, and position-
    ing (STP) marketing, 147.
    *See also* brand marketing
selective customer acquisition, 37–38
self-selection targeting, 21, 43, 45, 46
services
    in ARA marketing model, 148–154,
        159–160
    balancing and optimizing customer,
        137, 139, 140
    in fostering customer life cycle,
        15–16
    in maximizing customer asset value,
        6–7
    in promoting add-on selling, 96–97,
        98
        customer affinity and, 113, 114
        make-or-buy decisions regarding,
            115–117
    in promoting customer acquisition,
        49
    in promoting customer retention,
        72–75, 157–158
        at Amazon.com, 78–79
        improving retention programs in,
            80–81
Shapiro, Carl, 199
share of requirements, 69
silent attrition, 69
Silicon Valley, 197
slingshot acquisition, 40
Sloan, Alfred, 6, 49
Southwest Airlines, 110–111, 157
Spiegel, 21
*Sports Expert*, 97
Sports Expert Online, 97, 99–103, 104
statistical modeling
    of add-on selling, 120, 122–123, 200
    of customer acquisition, 25, 43, 45,
        59, 62–65
    of customer retention, 27, 92
stocks
    effects of customer equity on,
        161–162
    future trends in valuations of, 204
STP (segmentation, targeting, and
    positioning) marketing, 147.
    *See also* brand marketing

Strategic Alliance Partnership Program
(SAPP), 97, 99–103, 104
survival retention model, 86–87
SWAT team, 179
switching barriers, 10
in adaptive marketing, 130
with e-commerce, 198–199
in retaining customers, 74–75, 79

target marketing
in customer acquisition, 66
ACTMAN model of, 43–46, 50, 51
American Express Membership
Rewards as, 40–42
databases for, 55–56
in managing customer equity, 9–10
RFM analysis for, 17–18
teams
customer development management,
180–181, 185
structure of cross-functional, 177,
179
technology
future trends in, 193, 194, 196–197
in managing customer equity, 7–8
*See also* accounting systems; databases
telecommunications industry
add-on selling in, 96
brand equity in, 205
television ads, 46, 50–51
"Tell It Like It Is" (McGraw), 114
third-degree targeting, 21, 43, 45, 46
3M, 176
*Time*, 111, 112
Time Life Books, 55, 111
Total Quality Management, 10
Toyota, 85
transaction customers, 70
trials, 48–49, 51

United Airlines, 110
Universal Card (AT&T), 96
UPS, 110
USAA, 205
U.S. Armed Forces, 50–52
U.S. Census Bureau, 45

value (defined), 72, 73
Varian, Hal R., 199
virtual corporations, 202–203
*Vogue*, 112

Wal-Mart, 67, 200
"What I Know for Sure" (Winfrey),
114
winback prices, 47
Winfrey, Oprah, 111, 112–115
Wurster, Thomas, 77
W.W. Grainger, 74
www.customerequity.com
accounting measures for customer
equity at, 23, 24
computing customer acquisition at,
52
customer equity balance sheet at, 165
optimizing customer equity measures
at, 134

Yahoo!, 96, 115, 117–118
yield management pricing, 70

Zantac, 156
ZapMail, 109
Zap Online, Inc., 19–20
zip code response rates, 45
Zukav, Gary, 114

# About the Authors

***Robert C. Blattberg*** is the Polk Bros. Distinguished Professor of Retailing and the Director for the Center for Retail Management in the Kellogg Graduate School of Management at Northwestern University. Prior to accepting this position in 1991, he served as the Charles H. Kellstadt Professor of Marketing and the Director of the Center for Marketing Information Technology in the Graduate School of Business at the University of Chicago. He coauthored the book *Sales Promotions* and coedited *The Marketing Information Revolution*. Professor Blattberg specializes in database marketing, customer marketing strategies, retailing, and pricing. He serves as a Director of First Tennessee Bank Corporation (Memphis) and Price Chopper (Schenectady, New York).

***Gary Getz*** is Managing Principal and leader of the customer equity practice at Integral, Inc., a consulting firm dedicated to helping companies grow and create wealth in turbulent markets. Integral works in collaboration with noted faculty affiliates such as Bob Blattberg and Jakki Thomas to bring leading-edge business concepts into practical, and profitable, use. Mr. Getz has appeared on CNN, NPR, and Bloomberg Television, and has published several articles on marketing and strategy topics. Prior to joining Integral, he led strategy consulting practices at Strategos and The MAC Group/Gemini Consulting. He lives in Portola Valley, California, with his wife and two cats.

***Jacquelyn S. Thomas*** is Assistant Professor of Marketing at Emory University in Atlanta, Georgia. Prior to joining Emory, she received her Ph.D. in marketing with an emphasis in econometrics from Northwestern University and was a marketing professor at Stanford University. Dr. Thomas specializes in developing and applying models that enhance customer relationship management strategies. Prior to becoming a professor, she worked in the pharmaceutical industry with Merck Inc. She is married to a very supportive husband and they are blessed with a beautiful daughter and a German shepherd.